# ANSWERING GOD'S CALL TO WRITE

Yolanda Chen aka Wen-Hui Yiu

ISBN 979-8-89130-504-5 (paperback)
ISBN 979-8-89130-505-2 (digital)



Christian Faith Publishing
832 Park Avenue
Meadville, PA 16335
www.christianfaithpublishing.com

Printed in the United States of America

# Contents


Introduction..................................................................................v

The Motivation of My Writing Ministry ...........................................1
How God Brought Me to US with USD 1.25.............................22
I Was Baptized by the Holy Spirit...................................................41
The True Story of Another Adoption.............................................53
Completely Surrender before God, Part 1......................................75
Completely Surrender before God, Part 2......................................82
Completely Surrender before God, Part 3....................................104
Completely Surrender before God, Part 4....................................117

# Introduction

When God calls us, He also equips us. He provides His presence, His power, and everything we need. The main core theme of the book is "Completely surrender before God." The key element, I responded with the same willing obedience and attitude totally, absolutely with all my heart. Through it all, in the end, despite all my weaknesses and all my obstacles that I had inevitably faced. I give my heartfelt thanks to *you* for helping me amazingly finish this extraordinary work. Thank you, Lord. You deserve my full obedience and worship. *You* alone deserve all the praises and the glory!

> He who began a good work in you will carry it
> on to completion until the day. (Philippians 1:6)

To Him be the glory!

# The Motivation of My Writing Ministry

In general, when people get older, some of them, especially those who have been successful in business and what they have achieved is extraordinary in contributions to their clans, families, and communities, or society, they want to write something about their successful achievements and distinguished contributions of the significant works in their lives. As I am writing this, in my surroundings, I have seen a few people are doing that. What's the purpose?

I have overheard that the main idea is to be remembered, to be acknowledged for who they are by their families, younger generations to come—of course, by friends, communities, and society. It's commonly understood and accepted as the nice thing to do. It also may have some inspirational contribution as a good model and positive influence. Overall, their impact will be helpful, beneficial, and encouraging to the younger generations as well. I would say that there is nothing wrong with those who are inclined to do so, but I think that is not always the case. I am sure that there are also other people who do good things for different purposes or motivations.

Conversely, sometimes there are some people who don't always want to be acknowledged or noticed. They may be quietly doing things under God's calling or convictions regardless of the size of the works and being noticed or not. I think that they may be the unsung heroes of the society or of the world, but not in God's sight. God in His ways and His time frame will richly reward them in His very special way.

While I was writing this, I read one of Moody Bible Institute's devotional guides. One of the articles brings a question for the readers: have you ever experienced the call of God in your life? One of the answers is sometimes we are specifically given a particular assignment simply for His glory. When I read that, I didn't immediately know why I have thought about my writing. It seems to fit this question. Apply this to the precious lesson that I had learned previously: "Completely surrender before God." As for me speaking, my answer is simply in responding to His call and His conviction with a humble and submissive heart and attitude. Yes, learn from Pastor Chuck Swindoll's sound application tip of putting the truth into practice. I remember that Pastor Chuck also has said in a humorous way that when God calls you, you can only answer, "Yes, Lord!" No room to argue. I like that. Obviously, as sure as I agree with what Pastor Chuck has said, I want to surrender to His calling and plan as my way of obeying His grand plan and His design for me in my life.

At first, for a period of time, I had been seriously praying, deeply thinking through the days and meditating on God's Word to seek His will to not misunderstand and confuse God's calling or conviction. I was constantly listening and waiting for His answer and confirmation.

Practically speaking, I think that beforehand, I need to share the story behind all the stories I am going to share. Regarding the writing issue, I feel I must give serious thinking and evaluate the main thing and a few small issues. In general, I know for a fact that I am not qualified to do such a long, time-consuming, important work as writing. It is quite a heavy weight sort of work. I considered myself a very busy person most of the time. Quality and quantity of time and worry are my number one concern. Where can I find the time for doing such a significant long-term work? Therefore that it's not for me.

Apparently, I am hesitating and resisting to accept for a few practical reasons. Besides the time, a few other issues that I considered as important, such as technical computer-usage-issue requirements, came to mind. They are very important issues: language and technical Internet skills. English is not my own mother language, so it's not going to be easy. For sure, I know that I need one or two people who can be in partnership with me to help in the long-term writing process. Because it is a long-time commitment, it'd be too much to ask people for this kind of help. I'd say that these kinds of concerns are legitimate and necessary. Yes, these will be a big challenge in the process of the working on the writing journey.

Anyhow, what's the solution? While in the waiting period, simply keep on praying, asking, and listening for His answer and confirmation. On the other hand, there are another few small, legitimate issues that I need to give consideration as well. Well, with all those things swirling in my mind, it seemed too many negative thoughts and attitudes in the way are hindering me from making the right decision.

I think there is a difference between legitimate concerns and worry. I feel that I am struggling with having both legitimate concerns to the point of worrying—or both at the same time. That kind of attitude indicates the sign that little faith has been still debating in my heart. Interestingly, one day, I accidently found something from my own notes. It's from Pastor Jon Courson's teaching on the radio. He said that God doesn't use qualified people; He qualifies those whom He wants to use. *Wow!* What a great insight and a powerful encouragement! I think that this is a perfect reminder in time of my praying, searching, and waiting. After all, I also have thought about that a long time ago when I was working on a program to receive a certificate as a member of American Association of Christian Counselors (AACC). It's developed by the Center for Biblical Counseling Ministry. Their ministry is to teach the church how to care for people in God's way. It's a very practical program.

I remember one of the courses had mentioned that there are three major principles emphasized in regard to working in God's ministry. First, doing God's ministry or work must be a calling from God. Since it is a calling from God, we must pray fervently with a heart attitude of obedience, to make sure that the ministry is God calling you and appointing you to do so. Sometimes it's easy to become confused or it is hard to clarify and distinguish between what's God's will and what is from our own personal emotional feelings.

Second, after all, since you know that it is God's calling or conviction, you have to learn to actually depend on Him in practical ways, which means praying through all along the way to make sure you are continually engaging with His Spirit and will. In other words, your confidence should be based on His provisions, His unlimited resources. The key is that God's work must be done God's ways.

Third, seriously and deeply understand that it's God's design and His will to put you to do His work so that you will do it all for the purpose for Him alone. In essence, naturally and ultimately, He is the only one you worship and serve and also the only one to praise, to honor, and *who* deserves all the glory.

With those great insightful points of view and the theoretically based perspective, it's really restrengthening my desire and submission to His will. Keep in mind, be aware and be patient that the challenges will occur from time to time. In essence, despite any obstacles and hardships during the midst of the process, I need to develop a solid, strong faith in Him and deeply engage with His spiritual strength constantly all along the way instead of worrying about those hang-ups and being negative minded. I commit myself and will continue to live by "faith, not worry and fear." I seriously think hard and know that the God who has given me mighty strength and has brought me to this day is the same God who will continue to sustain me for whatever I need in the process to make it through my day every day. Very thankful for His assurance and promise in 1 Corinthians 10:13: God won't let us carry the burden more than we can bear. If that happens, He will always help us to find a way out for us (my paraphrase). Okay?

One day in my quiet time, I read these passages, thinking and meditating hard, that our heavenly Father, who created all things, the whole universe, He did it simply with His words. One word from Him and His amazing power is evident. The Bible says,

> As the rain and the snow, come down from
> heaven, and do not return to it without watering
> the earth…so is my word that goes out from my
> mouth. It will not return to me empty, but will

accomplish what I desire, and achieve the purpose for which I sent it. (Isaiah 55:10a, 11)

Praise the Lord for His powerful scriptures as a profound reminder to me at this crucial issue and encourage me to make the right decision as well.

As a matter of fact, the following true story is another actual incident directly motivating me to get started to write recently. The background was when we first moved to Riverside, California. We were introduced by Pastor McGrew in Hillside Free Methodist church in Evanston, Illinois, to attend the Riverside Free Methodist church. There was a very nice, devoted Christian leader who had gone to Taiwan to establish a theological seminary in southern part of Taiwan, Kaohsiung, the second largest city in Taiwan. His name was Byron Lamson, who was a professor in a seminary school. He was a theologian, pastor, teacher, and author of few books. Dr. Lamson was a very humble man, though he had many titles. He also had a great sense of humor, a very respectful Christian leader. He went to meet the Lord at the good age of ninety-seven years old. I loved him dearly and liked him a lot. We also lived very close to each other, only a mile away. We were good friends and good neighbors as well.

One day I told him that I had written a few articles, which were individual stories. I would say that each single story was a beautiful, amazing story. Instead of calling them my stories, I would rather say that they were the stories that were given from God. The real irony is that He is the Author, main character, the ultimate designer, and planner behind every single story. In other words, I would honestly say that without God's empowering strength and working secretly behind them, there were no such amazing stories at all in the first place. I suppose I can also say that those were the amazing testimonies of God's miracle work that had occurred in my lifetime. Those encounters truly testify how God's miraculous amazing help surpassed all the challenges at each step of the process and every single step away.

When Dr. Lamson returned to me those articles that I gave to him to read, he told me, "Yolanda, you are a good writer."

I asked him, "Why did you say that?"

He answered, "Because your stories made me cry! Keep on writing. I also want to tell you that I like the way you talk, very charming."

What encouraging comments and positive attitude. That really meant a great deal to me! Through it all, the encounter with Dr. Lamson's incident happened around forty years ago. After all, since then, my life had been too rough. Too many difficult issues have happened constantly. In general, I came to the point that the complex circumstances had overwhelmed me, and I don't have time and effort to think about anything else. Therefore, the writing issue has been completely forgotten, even out of my mind and thoughts.

In the middle of 2021, in the midst of COVID-19, the pandemic was spreading scary and crazy. Our general activities were very much restricted to the point that required us to stay home. Lots of stores were forced to shut down, even no services in the churches. In general, our lifestyle radically changed.

One day, during my quiet time, I was studying God's Word when something unusual happened out of the blue. I usually have my own devotional materials, such as Searchlight Ministry (with Pastor Jon Courson) playing on the radio and Pastor Courson's application commentary. There was another main material, *Today in the Word* (a production of the ministry of Moody Bible Institute), in addition to a few of my favorite devotional guides. All of those resources have a high regard for God's wisdom and teaching in theology and its application. Interestingly enough, I couldn't tell that exactly from what specific messages which touched me specifically. All I remember was that I just loved and enjoyed all of the materials I read. It's not merely knowing the information or understanding doctrinal teachings. I felt that it's beyond only enjoying the study, an—d I had a desire like to read more and more. It even felt hard for me to stop studying, and I didn't even want to get up from the carpet. I was simply enjoying and soaking in the deep thoughts. In my life, I have never experienced getting drunk with wine, only being drunk with His Spirit.

Just in that amazing moment, I felt that my heart and my soul were deeply engaging with His spirit and felt the special closeness with the intimate relationship with my Lord. Those were indescribable, sweet, precious moments I treasured in my heart very deeply. It was at that very special moment that I was triggered and reminded of many previous miraculous incidents, which are amazing stories of what happened in my life. I didn't know why I felt like I didn't want to get up but kept on pondering and soaking in those thoughts and sweet moments.

In essence, this brought me back, triggered my thoughts, and brought my attention to the desire to writing, which had been completely forgotten. The more I thought about those unforgettable, amazing stories, the stronger my desire to write became. I felt good about the decision I made; I thought that it was a God-given desire and His timing. I sensed the call to proclaim the gospel by returning to writing as a form of ministry, the long and completely forgotten writing issue in my busy life. Through all those good messages, somehow, the Holy Spirit nudged or convicted in my heart. Suddenly, it just rekindled my mind and thoughts and intensified my thoughts to write. It firmly, surely decided to do the writing ministry as my way to worship Him and humbly to obey to His call as well.

It's really hard to express my inner emotional feelings. In my life, I have never experienced getting drunk with wine, only being drunk with His Spirit and Word. That kind of satisfaction and joy runs so deep in my heart, mind, and soul. At times, when that moment occurs in my time alone with my Lord, I don't even want to get up to face my activities, but sit at the same spot and keep thinking, pondering, and soaking in those thoughts and sweet, precious moments. Yes, indeed those sweet, solemn, and peaceful mind and thoughts brought me back, triggering my attention to remembering my writing and desire to restart again.

Another key element that motivated me was that I have also thought about that my whole life. I had constantly experienced so many hardships, a variety of challenges, pain, and difficulties that frequently overwhelmed my life. In the midst of those horrible, terrible times, I experienced firsthand God's compassion and actually received His supernatural help, comfort, and rescue. The ironic fact was that without His miraculous works and supernatural intervention at all times, I wouldn't be in this world, and I wouldn't have become the way I am now. In other words, the scriptures at 2 Corinthians 1:3–4: "The Father of compassion and the God of all comfort, who comforts us in all our troubles, so that we can comfort those in any trouble with the comfort we ourselves have received from God." This scripture is the prefect description that expresses and describes my life situations. That's also the vital part of the reasons that nudged me to write. The focal point is that it's all based on the powerful Word of God. The Word is Jesus Himself. As John 1:1 says it perfectly, "In the beginning was the Word and the Word was with God, and the Word was God." Everything was made by Jesus Christ, even this day (John 1:3). Jesus said, "I and Father are one" (John 10: 30). It's all about Jesus. He is at the center of my heart and has become everything in my life. Here is an insightful truth from *My Utmost for His Highest*: "The key to the missionary's work, you must know Jesus yourself!" Indeed, as is always the center theme of this writing and the only purpose is exalting the authority of Jesus.

Father, God, thank You for Your love and for calling me to be a part of sharing the good news with the world.

As we may have heard that when a hungry beggar finds the food, the gourmet food, he can't wait to tell the other beggars where to find the food. The same is true that here I am, by the grace of God. I have been very blessed with the honor to be chosen and to know our Lord Jesus Christ. And my whole life, I have experienced firsthand God's numerous miracles after the miraculous incidents. I couldn't just selfishly enjoy and benefit for myself only. Such a most important issue in our lives, I can't just keep it to myself anymore. I can't wait to spread it out as soon as possible in the way God wants me to.

Likewise, the beggar is eagerly and excitingly ready to tell the other beggars where to find the food, the nutritious food. Besides, it's much more than the simple food. It's the *best food* of the best. It not only satisfies your physical needs, it also nourishes, cherishes, and cultivates your mind, thoughts, and soul—a combination of all three at the same time for the rest of your life. This particular special gourmet food is found in *Jesus Himself alone*. Through it all, the beggar who first actually tasted the good news and truly inhaled and exhaled with his own mouth and nose now has a great passion burning in his heart to share that supernatural food.

The same is true of me. It's my deepest motive and honor to eagerly share the supernatural food with other beggars. I have heard that there is a saying, "Let all the chips fall where they may." I am praying that God will let those stories do the speaking and preaching to wherever God leads. May those God-given miraculous stories fall to the place where they should, and may that be under God's way and God's leading.

As a matter of the fact, while I started to write, a few people have asked me, "Are you writing for money or for fame?"

I firmly responded with honesty and dignity, "Neither and never, not even 1 percent of the truth." After all, at times I have pondered, been perplexed, and questioned myself about this question. "Since the encounter with Dr. Lamson has gone by for so long. He had gone with the Lord a long time ago."

On the other hand, the reality is that I am getting older and weaker in many respects. I want to live a retired-person lifestyle, such as not many commitments, relaxed, no hurry, kick-back mindset, feeling not guilty for "doing nothing." That will be a big revolutionary issue to me. For sure, I felt like the Lord, my Master, was firmly saying to me, "Retire? Not so soon. Wait until I say so." As Pastor Chuck Swindoll said, the only answer to Him is, "Yes, Lord!" Period!

Sometimes I'd like to figure out about why that has been waiting for forty years long and why God still wants me to do it! It'd be much easier to just let go of it, put it behind for good. But I am convinced that God still wanted me to do it rather than give up on me. Sometimes, when I felt I wanted to give up, I felt guilty and uncomfortable in my mind and heart. Timewise, it doesn't sound right. I have heard that Jesus rarely comes when we expect Him. *He appears* when we least expect Him and always in the most illogical situations or wrong timing. In fact, due to COVID-19, this is crazy radical time to the whole world and to me as well. As always, the only way is to remain obedient to His timing and ways.

Despite all those legitimate concerns, don't I believe that God knows and cares? Being very honest for a while, I have been hesitating, struggling about my decision, even though my mind has determined to do it. But I think about those realities, challenges that I have to go through. I think that the mixed feelings of the undecided thoughts and complex issues still couldn't settle down. They have been bothering me and troubling my heart frequently.

I think that I agreed with what Alexander Whyte has said that the Christian life is basically a series of new beginnings. How true that is. In our lifelong journey, we will always stumble and fall and feel downcast in spite of how we think we are strong and pious or devoted to God. But the truth is that the Bible says so too. This is what Jesus has said: "In this world you will have trouble. But take heart. I have overcome the world" (John 16: 32). In other words, in our lifetime, challenges will always be inevitable. But if we truly believe in Him, whatever the challenges we face, they will always be overcome because of Him. Therefore, our faith in Jesus is all we need. Faith is a positive attitude of proactiveness, so it's up to us to see how strong a faith we have in Jesus.

As in the previous incident, Pastor McGrew had told me in the very beginning that God has His grand plan for each one of us, and He answers our prayers in His time and ways. In fact, I have to constantly remind myself about it. The Bible says, "There is a time for everything, and a season for ever activity under heaven" (Ecclesiastes 3:1). In essence, God always knows what He is doing before it even comes to pass. Looking back from the Bible story in Genesis 12:1, 2, and 4, God had told Abram to depart from his own country, own clans, and his family. A Bible commentator believes he was about fifty years old when he initially heard God's call, but he didn't leave until he was seventy-five years old. According to this commentator, Abram faltered in his obedience. But waiting until twenty-five years later, it came to pass. God still didn't give up on Abram; rather, He waits for Abram.

The same is true with me. God wasn't mad at me for my procrastination, neglect, and little faith. He neither gave up on me nor stopped me from continuing to write. On the contrary, He has used different ways of telling me, nudging me. He waited for forty years for His own purpose and plan, which I didn't really know why. Yet I still have a strange peace and am still willing to obey His agenda because I trust that His plan or will is always the best for His plans in the future, which only He knows.

There was another episode or true illustration that also goes along with this issue. While Pastor McGrew was first visiting in our house at Skokie, Illinois, I remember vividly our conversation. He mentioned the idea of *adoption* and had given the biblically based viewpoint. He said, "We are all created from the same God, and someday, we will go to the same God, so what's the difference between your child and my child!?"

How true! So true and beautiful! Although I was so touched and admired His godly insight at the time, I think it was at the wrong timing at the time that was why even I heard about it—adoption— but didn't mean anything to me. Until it was in due season, in God's perfect timing, while even after I really, actually have learned the lesson of "Completely surrender before God."

And I even had asked Him this particular question in my prayer: "Lord God, after all, You have already changed our hearts from 100 percent *no* to 100 percent *yes* [about adoption]. And it has taken about ten months or one year for both of us to thoroughly learn to accept the fact of the *adoption*. So what is the next that *You* have for us to do?"

Amazingly enough, it's in that perfect timing God has used His unique ways to nudge me and convict me to pay attention about the *adoption* matter. In general, I consider myself as a simple, naive, and unsophisticated person. Living in a kind of free and casual lifestyle, not too many things are serious to me in many areas or respects. There is one exception, which is that I firmly stick to the uncompromised truth of God's Word, regardless in any respects.

*Concluding thoughts*

First, I felt a tremendous, great honor and privilege to be chosen or called as a humble servant or chosen instrument. On the other hand, I take great joy working on it. What a blessing that I am still able to testify and to share those miraculous stories that only God can perform through me. Such an unworthy, ordinary, lowly sinner like me also can be used by Him. That's amazing!

Second, how true—so true—that He has proven Himself as a faithful ultimate provider, sustainer who actually actively is working in the midst of the journey process. I see Him at work all along the way in the public place or behind the scenes. In the very secret small corner and even at every turning of any circumstances. The detail of the process has happened since the very beginning through the very end. The real irony was that without His actually working behind the whole picture, there is no picture at all in the first place—period!

Lastly, only He alone deserves all the honor and the glory, which He would share with no one on earth or in the whole universe. He said that "I am the Lord your God…you shall have no other gods before me" (Exodus 20:2, 3), and "You shall not bow down to them or worship; for I, the Lord your God, am a jealous God" (Exodus 20:5).

I truly count it a privilege and honor to be chosen by God to do the telling-the-other-beggars-to-know-Jesus ministry. As Pastor Greg Laurie has said how he first started his ministry without having had any theology background or equipping and training as a seminary student. This is what he has said in his preaching: "I simply tell people the Jesus whom I know." Simply with that kind of personal, genuine experiences, his preaching already attracted lots of followers. He first started his ministry at a very young age. God has richly blessed him and his ministry for proclaiming the Jesus whom he has known. The lesson of the application for me to learn is that with the maximum talents He has given me and with what I have in my hand, I serve Him.

I also learned the story from Moses when he was still arguing with God from his feeling of inability to be used by God. God asked him, "What do you have in your hand?"

He answered, "A cane!"

Regarding Moses's example, since it's God's specific grand plan for Moses, regardless of Moses's issues about being incapable. In the end, God Almighty will always accomplish what He started. In fact, what God required of him was his totally obedient heart and attitude. The rest was God's business, even though all he had was a cane. As for me, although I had desire to write, but in reality, with no writing experiences, and many other hang-ups, and feeling of inadequacy of serving.

Yet when I put this in God's sight, I see that all I need to do is submit my total willingness and practice the best I can with my God-given ability. He will supply and provide everything I need to accomplish His plan for me. But simply by sharing or telling people the way from my own life experiences as the first person who lives with the pain and works at answers through God's mighty power. After all, in appreciation of revering and obeying His calling about the writing ministry, I sincerely committed myself to writing the uncompromised truth of God's Word and truth.

As I always mentioned in the stories, at the core of everything I do, I say that focus on Jesus our Lord in the top front and top center in our daily life, on purpose to live out our true Christian identity as God's firm believers and servants. What does it mean to live out our Christian identity and the Spirit-filled life? By changing our life, our lifestyles, characters, and conducts in our daily activities. In other words, what I've learned is to preach and to share the gospel everywhere with the best of God's given ability and opportunity.

And to prove it with my transformational character and conduct as the evidence not only at church but also in my home, work arenas, surroundings, and communities as well. As a matter of fact, I just remember a true story that had happened while I was in Taiwan a few years ago. While I was taking a taxi, I initiated the conversation with the taxi driver, which was motivated by my inner desire to share the gospel with him. This act was driven by my transformed conduct (because this act wasn't my natural, normal character). Before I opened my mouth, I prayed to the Holy Spirit for the courage, the boldness, and the wisdom how to start the conversation. On the other hand, I prayed for the Holy Spirit to open his heart to listen as well.

To make a long story short, I started asking a couple of questions, and he impatiently answered me. I simply ignored and accepted his uncooperative attitude. I continued to talk to him and thanked him for his reply. I then started to get to the point, and I said that I am a Christian believer in Jesus, and this is the best blessing and most important thing in my life, briefly sharing with him about the fundamental basic truth about Christianity: "whosoever believes in Him" (John 3:16). Not only my eternal life is secured, but in this life, I have someone to depend upon, someone I can totally trust, and never will He abandon me. Jesus's love and acceptance are unconditional fact. Not only does the Bible say so, but I also personally actually experienced it.

Regardless, he asked, "How do you know?"

I broke myself honestly and sincerely shared a few terrible experiences of my heartache, previous pain, sadness, frustration, anger, hardships, etc. My paraphrase from John 16:33: In this world, you are going to have troubles, all kinds of setbacks. Some are from natural disasters, and others from evil people's bad behaviors, but since I have overcome the world, therefore, those who believe in me will overcome the world as well.

I shared with him, simply out of kindness, like the beggar's story that I have found what is the best and most important thing and wanted to share with him. That's the main idea. Guess what! From his unwilling or impatient attitude to listen in the beginning, to my surprise, before I had to take off from his car, the way he reacted to me was much more friendly, nicer, and he even kindly helped me unload my stuff from the car and even thanked me for the sharing. I encouraged him go to the church near where he lives. I can't control what's after, but I considered that the opportunity for me to plant the seeds. I hope someday, maybe some other people will continue to plant more and more in Taiwan.

Regarding the true character's meaning, the sixteenth president of the US, Abraham Lincoln, commented about character, "All men can stand in adversity, but to test the man's character only give them power."

Former president George W. Bush said, "I am using the power to help people." He also has other viewpoints, that true character connoted this meaning: "If you are the same person before the pulpit and behind the screen when nobody sees you. That's who you really are."

On the other hand, the Christian personal character should be also applied or practiced in tough times and easy times as well. While I am writing this article, there's a very special event I want to point out. We will never forget September 11, 2001. I would say that was the most tragic or saddest evil event in the modern history of our country. When the tragedy had just happened, President Bush was scheduled to spend time with a group of young children in a classroom. The secret serviceman suddenly walked into the classroom, whispering to his ear. His face drastically changed very seriously. He then said a few words to the students and then bowed his head and led all the kids and people in the classroom to pray before he left. I was very touched, surprised that in such a horrible, extremely important moment, he had boldness and even remembered to pray.

After the tragedy had come to pass, our country held a National Memorial Service at Crystal Cathedral Chapel to honor and remember those who had lost their precious lives in that tragedy. Pres. George W. Bush was sitting in the front pew, and his father president was sitting on the pew behind him. He lightly patted his son's shoulder and said to him, "Son, I am sorry that on this sad, critical event, I can't help you. You have to do it on your own."

Answer from the son president: "Dad, I am not alone. I have the Father God, who is helping me." He used his finger, pointing to the top.

From these two incredible incidents or episodes, former president George W. Bush really had demonstrated his very noble, beautiful acts and attitude as a brave leader of our country. That's also showing his strong personal Christian character not only as a great leader but also as a firm believer in Jesus Christ as well. Well done, Mr. President George W. Bush. God bless you for your steadfast faith in Him even in a time of such awful, sad, and tragic event!.

Pastor Greg Laurie has said, "If we can take care of our characters, God will take care of our reputations!" How true, so very true!

Matt Damon, Oscar-winning actor, producer, and screenwriter, said, "The definition of success is the process itself." He also shared that true fulfillment comes from loving what you do.

> It's really about feeling that I did my best work, feeling that we told the story we wanted to tell in the way we wanted to tell it. That is really the definition of success.

Great insight! I love it. I really like to say amen with it.

Helen Keller also has an in-depth perspective: "Character can't be developed in ease and quiet time. Only through the experience of trial and suffering can the soul be strengthened, ambition inspired, and success achieved."

The godly personal character does not come automatically. It requires a persistent diligent work and actual walking through the midst of the process. Despite that we are on the mountaintop or down in the valley, we should still firmly remain being humble with dignity. In other words, I mean that in spite of any circumstances, still remaining on the uncompromised truth of God. It's not easy and never will be. I just remember the powerful scripture from 2 Corinthian 4:7:

> We are afflicted in every way, but not crushed, perplexed, but not despairing; persecuted, but not forsaken, struck down, but not destroyed; always carrying about in the body the dying of Jesus, so that the life of Jesus also may be manifested in our body.

I would say that this biblical truth describes the attitude of Christian character when we encounter tough situations or unbearable burdens. The flip side, on the contrary, sometimes when we are in a place of exaltation, can we still remain in the same humble honest-with-dignity attitude?

I remember a true story a long time ago. I attended a church meeting where the speaker was a professional psychiatrist. When I first arrived in the room, I saw a lady with a very plain outfit and hairstyle. She was helping to put chairs out to get ready for the meeting. I was the second arriver in the room. I joined her and helped to put out the chairs too. From our conversations, I was surprised and realized that she will be the speaker in the meeting. I was very impressed about that kind of humble attitude, integrity, and conduct. She seemed just like one of the church members. I thought her acts and natural behavior connote her personal Christian character and demonstrated a real testimony to me before she talked. So called, walk the walk, not just talk the talk. Honestly, although I admired her, I didn't remember what she's talking about in the meeting, yet I vividly remember her humble personal character. As we all have heard, action speaks louder than words.

I once read a statement in an article from Oswald Chambers's devotional book *My Utmost for His Highest*. It says, "Christian workers' greatest need is a readiness to face Jesus Christ at any and every turn." Well said! Great perspective!

The greatest evangelist Dr. Billy Graham once said about personal character, "When you lost your money, you lost nothing. When you lost your health, you lost something. But when you lost your personal character, you lost everything!" What a profound insight as well.

As for me, the first and foremost, I must not only be kept right with God daily at all times: the vital, important issue is to continue to stay in spiritual harmony with God by developing and cultivating the inner purity in God's sight. It must depend on our solid personal character. The Bible says, "Blessed are the pure in heart, for they shall see God" (Matthew 5:8). It is the "pure in heart" who see God.

In the end, regarding my writing ministry, all the challenges and a few small hang-ups here and there, I try to learn to accept them and won't let them stop me. On the other hand, I really enjoy very much to work on it. It won't be easy for sure, but I think that as I have said previously, the true fulfillment comes from loving what you do. The ironic truth is that I am really enjoying and loving what I do, really feeling that I do my best work, feeling that I told the story the way I wanted to tell it. I didn't know why I felt good and had a great sense of freedom and boldness and a sense of satisfaction to share my true feelings without feeling intimidated.

I really want to appreciate that I am so blessed and lucky to live in this great country *America* the beautiful as an early immigrant from Taiwan. She gives me the right of freedom of speech. I feel that I shouldn't be simply selfish to take all the blessings for granted. I considered myself as one of the patriot citizens and want to participate and that's my way to show my appreciation as a citizen's obligation and responsibility. I feel that I want to say a few things from my heart to show my appreciation first to God's blessing to our country.

Second to those who are the brave patriot leaders of the Pro-America Leaders such as former president Donald Trump and Vice President Mike Pence and several other devoted leaders. They are all working very hard to stand strong to fight for protecting our country to "let America be America" as the way that our forefathers have started in the beginning. The former president Trump especially appreciated their strong leadership and unyielding commitment to continue to fight for our fundamental Christian faith in America. To defend and support our traditional Christianity values of our national motto: "IN GOD WE TRUST." President Trump extends special thanks to the Faith and Freedom Coalition for their diligent work on the front lines in defense of the dignity of life, marriage, and family. I'd like to quote Dr. Ben Carson's great insight: "Faith is not a dormant. I know some people have the attitude of 'Well, God's in charge.' But *He* uses us! So we have to be involved as well."

As a Christian, my attitude is always "Besides prayer, I always ask God, 'What can I do within my ability or availability to help or contribute to that particular matter?'" Honestly, it always turned out pretty interesting and amazing and surprised me too.

The following is the list of several significant quotes from our forefathers in the history:

America was Founded and Built on Faith in God. (Declaration of Independence, July 4, 1776)

Blessed is the nation whose God is the Lord. (Psalm 33:12)

God, who gave us life, gave us liberty. Indeed I tremble for my country when I reflect that God is just, that his justice cannot sleep forever. (Thomas Jefferson, author of America's Declaration of Independence, third president of America)

To the distinguished character of patriot, it should be our highest glory to add the more distinguished character of Christian. (Gen. George Washington, America's first president)

Where there is no law, there is no liberty. (Benjamin Franklin)

As Christians, the Bible calls us to be salt and light to influence our culture." (Dr. Ben Carson)

In America we know that faith and family, not the government and bureaucracy, are the center of the American life. Our motto is, "In God We Trust." (former president Donald J. Trump)

I remember that back when George W. Bush was running for the presidency, there was a senator (forgot his name). He said in the conference, "I can live without a country, but I can't live without a family." I'd say that any normal people would agree with that. Indeed, family is the basic, the important unit, also the only place for anybody to start our lives after we were born. Former president Trump has strong commitment to embrace on the vital parental roles value in the family.

When Mother Teresa received her Nobel Prize, she was asked, "What can we do to promote world peace?"

She replied, "Go home and love your family."

Love on earth begins at home. (Mother Teresa)

The definition of the success is the *process* itself in God's sight. Ultimately, thanks to the Lord for the great honor and privilege to serve Him the way He wanted me to. With His mighty strength and unlimited provisions, I know I will make it because He calls, He provides, and He helps all along the way! May *He alone* get all the praises and all the *glory!*

Lastly, I want to say it again that I am so privileged and honored to be used as God's chosen instrument to do this honorable project, writing. Now, I want to quote another key component to describe of the motive of my writing.

In the place God has put us he expects us to shine, to be living witnesses, to be a bright and shining light. While we are here our work is to shine for him. (Dwight L. Moody, founder, Moody Bible Institute)

Indeed, this quote is exactly depicting the whole purpose of this writing. And that's why I picked the title *Answering God's Call to Write*. That was exactly answering His call to write. The same is my attitude, as Mr. Moody's saying, "While I am here alive, my work is to shine for Him." May all the stories serve as the shining instruments to shine and to preach for themselves.

Now, I would like to quote an illustration, or parable, to conclude this article. I heard the parable during my Bible study with my favorite Pastor, Chuck Swindoll. He said that when a doctor is given a surgery to perform on a patient, he is required to wear gloves to do his job. But when he successfully finishes the surgery, he naturally takes off his gloves and throws them into the trash can. We all know that the one who performs the surgery is the doctor himself, not the gloves. Therefore, after the job is done, the gloves are no longer useful and go to the trash can; that's where the gloves belong.

The lesson I learned from this parable is that the doctor is a metaphor for God Himself, and we, as His servants, are the gloves. When God assigns us to do His work, in essence, He is the one who actually does the work, not us. We are only God's instruments. Whatever jobs God wants us to do, we should faithfully and loyally do as He wishes. But after we finish, we may feel satisfaction from the accomplishment. However, as the gloves, we ought to go to the trash can. We shouldn't take any credit from it or feel a sense of pride ourselves. The application to me is that whenever people admire me or say good words to me, I thank them for their kindness. Yet inside me, I never taken credit for it. Rather, I turn it over to the real Author and the actual Writer. Yes, it's good to hear people's kind words. However, in my heart, I always remember this illustration and clarify God's and my roles, or positions. I know for a fact that God is the one who does the work; He is the Doctor, and I am the gloves. On the other hand, I always thank God for the great impact of this insightful illustration, which reminds me and teaches me the right attitude. I am very thankful that I am fully aware of my role and my position—the gloves in the trash can. That's where I ought to be and belong.

Thank You, Lord, for helping me acknowledge thoroughly and with awareness of WHO You really are and for the total submission to Your authority and the only ownership in everything I do and have in this world.

# How God Brought Me to
# US with USD 1.25
# In Fact, Did I Really Come
# to US with USD 1.25?

> What he opens no one can shut, and what
> he shuts no one can open.
>
> —Revelation 3:7b

First and foremost, I would like to quote one of the two most powerful scriptures in the Bible. They are also my favorite verses as well. Revelation 3:7b:

> If the door God wants to open, regardless how hard you try, it simply won't open for you. On the contrary, if God wants to close, despite how hard you try, it's for sure will close it for you, period! (I paraphrased)

Another verse is in Psalm 47:3:

> Delight yourself in the Lord, and He will put that desire in your heart.

However, the most important reason is that because they are the central core of the theme in this story. These two scriptures were the key verses n God's grand divine plan for the story. In addition, there, was a quote that I thought was also significantly relative with the story as well. This special quote is describing a deep emotional feeling straight from my heart. Although it seemed a very little thing, it touched my emotional feeling a great deal. "The most modest form of *love* is *tender love*." I think that it carries a very deep emotional concern.

Back in 1970, my husband, Jacob, came to the United States as a student to pursue his graduate program. I was working in Taiwan and wasn't thinking or planning about going to the States. For a while, there were a few complicated reasons: long old unresolved family issues hanging on my head and in my life frequently. They caused me feelings of loneliness, uncertainty, depression, and insecurity.

Then I didn't know why the desire of going to the States to join him was getting stronger gradually and slowly. I was a Christian, though I wasn't a very mature, strong Christians at the time. Yet I knew that the only way was to begin with prayer. In fact, besides prayer, there was nothing I could do anyway. Back then, I went to a local Presbyterian church. Before too long, a few friends in the church-asked me about something like the going-to-America issue.

There was a nice, kind couple in the church. They were particularly concerned about me, and they thought that since I was all alone with no children, I should go to America to join my husband. I told them I couldn't go due to the many obstacles and problems, and I had none of the requirements. Not even one item or requirement was available to me. That made it very tough and impossible for me to even think about it.

The story started from that church through that compassionate, nice couple's idea and also through meeting a man in our church who had been working in a travel agency for a long time. He came to me and asked me lots of things regarding what to do and how to work things out by planning and preparing those practical and concrete documents and telling me more about the important procedures, etc. He even offered his help and wanted to help me every step of the way.

If I look back carefully at the entire episode, God was faithful to prove Himself exactly as He had planned even way before in the beginning. The evidence of the story very much confirmed the meaning of this scripture: "what I have said, that will I bring about; what I have planned, that will I do" (Isaiah 46:11). The real irony of the purpose of writing this as a story instead of writing this story as a memoir is that I would rather say that it's God's way of performing His miracles after miracles through this complicated, amazing story.

In other words, God has a plan for me. He has a purpose for my existence, future, and whole life. To live out or fulfill His purpose or plan for me, to be honest, I really had no idea of how or what to do. I didn't know what direction to head or to move to. During the time of praying, searching, and waiting, I didn't know how or what to do!

I didn't know why, but I thought about an American pastor. His name is Jim Z. He's also a missionary in a Christian organization in Taipei. He and his whole family had been living in Taiwan for a long time. I first met him from the English Bible study in YWCA. I have attended his Bible study frequently.

One day, out of the blue, I decided to visit him and talk to him about my issue and the burden in my heart. To be honest, I was pretty depressed at the time I went to visit him in his house. At first, he was suggesting to me about some ideas of how to work it out. One thing was for sure: he has great desire and a compassionate heart and an attitude that wanted to help me out of the difficult issues. And if it was necessary, he was also willing to go with me to the American embassy in Taipei, Taiwan. I briefly told him what the problems were based on what I have overheard.

Anyhow, it was a nice conversation, and it was also nice sharing my burdens as well. Before I departed from his house, he said something very powerful for encouragement and had also shown me the perfect scripture that was exactly what I needed to hear. "What he opens no one can shut, and what he shuts no one can open" (Revelation 3:7b). I am sure that it was the Holy Spirit who instructed him.

He then shared his comments along with this verse. He said to me, "Yolanda, it seems that all of the problems are not the problems at all. The point is not based on how hard your government is, how bad the problems are, or any other obstacles you are going to face. Just like this scripture says, if now is the time that God wants you to go to America to meet your husband, He will open the door no matter how hard or how difficult the problems—regardless!

"On the other hand, if now is not the right timing for you to go to America, then no matter how hard you try to open, it just won't work—period!"

Obviously, the point is that it completely, absolutely, and totally depends upon our mighty God's hand. He then prayed for me before I left.

Believe it or not, after we finished our prayers, I couldn't believe how I felt. My heavy feeling was amazingly opened up. I felt my cloudy sky, the depressed feelings before I went to his house, was suddenly cleared up, and the heavy burden in my heart was simply gone and disappeared. Those previous feelings of anxiety and worry, those negative feelings and thoughts, were totally replaced by total peace of mind and calm rest in my thoughts and soul. I had asked myself, "What happened? And what's wrong with me?"

Back then I wasn't a strong, mature Christian, and I didn't know much about the Bible. Though I was a kind of Bible-ignorant Christian back then, I truly know it because of how I deeply feel. I learned later that the Bible says that peace of heart and mind come only from Jesus. Jesus is the Prince of peace (Isaiah 9:6) and also one of the Holy Spirit's fruits (Galatians, 5:22–23).

It came to pass, even while I was still in his house, when I walked out of his house, I noticed that the sky was beautiful blue as the way it has always been. The strange thing was that wasn't the color I saw before I went to his house. My mind kept on dwelling with the key verse, "If the door that God wants to open now, no matter how difficult it is" God will open it Himself! So it is completely up to Him alone!

This unique, awesome *scripture* has been glued and stayed in my heart and mind ever since then even to this day (Revelation 3:7b).

Thank You, Lord, for Your wonderful *Word!* What a sharp difference before and after I went to Pastor Jim Z.'s house. After all, I truly realized that the total peace and my confidence came straight from the ultimate source of God's Word and His Spirit. Indeed, it is so very true that Your *Word* is powerful. One word from You, and Your power is evident. I am simply in awe and amazed by *You.*

In the practical way of reality, the whole process was started from that kind, nice couple in the church who paid special attention to me and even acted upon this. They introduced me to the man who was working for the travel agency. (Though we were in the same church, to be honest, I didn't know him at all.) At times, I was pondering and puzzled. If I put it in slow motion, these small acts seem insignificant, common things to do. As I have mentioned earlier, "the definition of success means the process itself." Great insight! But on this particular case, that's exactly God's way to open the door for me, and He directed me how to start working on the very first step in the process of the whole procedure. The irony is true. Again, I could see that God was actually working at every turn or even in the very small steps of those details.

When I was writing this article, I was reminded of the matter of God paying attention to me. It was about a week before, during my Bible study about Joseph's story. I have thought about something that was similar to the behavior or act that happened in Joseph's life while he was put in jail. The long background was in Geneses 40:1 to 41:9–16. We know well that Joseph was put in jail because he was unjustly accused of succumbing to Potiphar's wife's demand. He was totally an innocent person. In the story, there were two very important persons: the cupbearer and the baker of the king of Egypt. The three of them were confined in the same prison cell. One day, Joseph came to them and asked them, "Why is your face so sad today?" The brief story was written in chapter 40:6.

The key essence was that it's from Joseph's extraloving concerns and his compassionate heart that noticed that their faces were so sad. Paying attention, he even asked questions why. We know the long story was about their strange dreams, and Joseph offered himself to help them interpret the meaning of their dreams. God had given and granted Joseph a special wisdom and intelligence of the interpretation of their dreams. Unfortunately, the chief cupbearer had completely forgotten about Joseph until two years later (Geneses 41:9).

The point of this story I learned is that although Joseph's being in jail was absolutely by wrong accusation, instead of complaining, pouting, or self-pitying his innocent case and fate, he was still kind enough to pay attention to other people's well-being. On the other hand, he didn't act superior to others even though he thought he had a higher position and was completely innocent, unlike other prisoners. In other words, he acts just like the rest of the prisoners and treats them equally. That's the quality of his true humility with dignity! In a way, the fact was that despite the wrong reason, Joseph was put in the same prison.

This story reminded me about a true story of my encounter that happened many years ago. I was working as an on-call interpreter for an interpreting company in San Bernardino, California. One time, my assignment was to a men's institution. In plain terms, it was a men's jail. I didn't know until I got there. Security was extremely serious, and although there were two big security guards or policemen who walked with me on my both sides, I still felt insecure and afraid. When I first walked into the actual jail building, I saw a very interesting poster on the wall that said, "We may all come from different boats, but now, we are all in the same boat." I thought that this humorous poster's words had very much the same idea that I am describing about Joseph in jail with other prisoners. I like to share what I thought was kind of funny and interesting. As I mentioned earlier in another article, it's really about the feeling that I did my best work, feeling that I told the story I wanted to tell in the way I wanted to tell it.

Back to the story, when I left Pastor Jim's house with a perky and happy mood, I was full of hope and joy spiritually and emotionally as well. In comparison to the time before I entered his house, which was only about one hour before. But coming out of his house, my feeling was completely different, and my attitude was much more confident. It was absolutely opposite from when I first came to his house.

After I left Pastor Jim's house, I went straight to my parents' house and told my mother that I would go to America about six months later. I really didn't know why, didn't even remember that I said that until my mother said to me, "You will be lucky if you can go to America. By the way, why did you say that you can go in about six months?"

All of a sudden from her questioning me, I asked myself the same question: why did I say that? To this day, I still vividly remember that I really had no idea why I said that, and it's more likely that I didn't even remember that I said that at all! It seems that I said it subconsciously, without knowing what I said and why I said it. In short, this was one of the very small details. Amazing—that strange act wasn't my plan at first. No clues! The only answer was the same as my previous mysterious stories: it was under God's directions and guidance.

Guess what? More bizarre or strange things are yet to come when the story finally comes to the end, the very end, when all the required documents and every step of the process were literally, actually finished and done completely and totally. Guess how long it took? Six months—period!

Again, naturally, you and I will ask the same question: how can that be? I think we all can't deny that's exactly the evidence of God's way to fulfill His plan and His design. His word: "If God wants to open the door, no one can shut it, on the contrary, if it's God's will to shut, no one can open it" (Revelation 3:7b, I paraphrased). Mysterious, isn't it? When I think hard and deep, I know that this incident had happened way before the nice couple in the church asked the travel agent's help on my behalf.

In regard to those six important requirements, the travel agent had been very patiently instructing me and telling me what to do step-by-step. Those official documents were really very complicated, and I needed to do lots of work. I have been very busy, running to several different government departments. In the beginning, the travel agent told me that he could help me only with the first five steps. He honestly told me that I could count on him for the first five steps, but the last step of the procedure was the hardest and also the most important step. The point was that without the last step, all of the previous works would go in vain—for nothing. In other words, although we made it through the first five issues, without getting through the last step, it would just ruin the whole issue for nothing. That would have been very sad, frustrating, angry, and disappointing.

During our work on the issue, when I went through every single step, I was very thrilled and happy. I always went to a friend's house and told her and her parents about the good news and how it was working, things like that. I had been doing that just about every single step when it went through. The true story of each incident was always difficult and complicated.

Again, I really knew that it was God's mighty hand working behind the steps. Even my friend's parents were very devoted Buddhists. They always liked to hear my report from those amazing, interesting encounters. Coming to the point, one time, when I was telling them the miraculous details during those steps, her father couldn't stop himself and confessed and told me, "It was your God who helped you out."

The friend's father—I called him *uncle*—I think he acknowledged that the God in whom I believe was the true God, but he was too prideful to admit it. So it was interesting that the uncle (friend's father) commented about how it was my God's help that I was able to go through all of those challenges. Of course, I had been praying not only every day but also in every situation. I was the first person walking through and working through all the processes. I could thoroughly, deeply testify that it's my dear Lord who was the actual *Person* working behind the scenes. How could I ignore it? How could I neglect it? And how could I forget to thank Him?

Time flies, and all of the five steps of the complicated hard work were finally just about completely finished. Thank God for all the help, either tiny, upfront, or behind the scenes. In spite of any circumstances, they all came to pass. Now, what's next?

I was waiting for the unknown answer for the most important crucial issue in the process. During the time when I was still waiting and didn't know what to do, I remembered something I had to do before I went to America. Jacob had asked his colleague to buy a rice cooker for him, and he owed his coworker fifteen US dollars. And of course, this was the best time to do what I wanted to do. I remember that Pastor Jon Courson said that whenever you don't know what to do, do what you know to do, and then you will know what to do. That's very true; great insight as well. In so doing, since I didn't know what to do at that time, I chose to do what I knew to do.

One day, I called his coworker and told him that I wanted to pay him on behalf of Jacob's rice cooker. He said, "Don't worry about it."

But I insisted. Then he said that he wanted to take me out to dinner. Since I had to meet him anyway, I said to him, "Okay."

We met in a beautiful restaurant, and we had not seen each other for a long time. At dinnertime, naturally, out of the kindness and concerns, he asked me how the process was going and how much was left to go at this point. I told him what the agent had told me about the procedure, that at this point, we had already finished every single step. We had made all of the required parts of the process, except the last step, which was the most important and also the hardest, critical step. Because without that particular special step, there was no way I could make it for my trip.

He, of course, asked me what that was. (He was simply asking out of his great concern.) I then told him exactly what I was told by the agent about the required document. Guess what I heard from him. Almost immediately, he put his hand on his chest. (That body language was telling me, "Not a problem." I can count on him—period!) In the meantime, he said to me, "No problem. The man who is in charge of this particular case is my roommate."

I was totally shocked and speechless, and I looked at him and said…nothing. I got goose bumps. I was simply in awe. I didn't know what to say!

How amazing because this was the most significant, critical issue, which even the special agent said to me in the very beginning that he couldn't do because it was beyond his ability. I still vividly remember his comment about this particular difficult situation. In addition, he even said that unless you had some kind of special connection with someone, he couldn't do it for me. The right solution was that I needed a special connection, but the question and the problem was, "Where could I find that kind of special connection?"

We have an expression that seems like, "I was searching for the needle in the ocean." As the words express clearly, it was impossible for me. But on this very special night, God provided it right before me at the perfect time. How amazing that on this special case, God already knew that I couldn't find it, and He knew I didn't know where to find it. In His perfect timing, His own unique, miraculous way, He provided it for me right in my presence. What an awesome God He is!

This is the real view, the whole view of our God to me. Regardless, He is at all times omnipotent, omnipresent, and omniscient. I confess that there are still a lot of things that I don't understand, but despite whatever reasons, I still want to trust Him and believe Him wholeheartedly. The almighty God in whom I believe is capable of healing all diseases, parting the seas, and even raising the dead to life. The great God He has been, and He is still great and wonderful today. Thank You, Lord, for helping me to find the perfect connection at the perfect timing! As the psalmist says, "You are my rescuer in the present time of my trouble" (I paraphrased from Psalm 46:1). And as my friend's father said to me, "It is your God who helps you out!" Interestingly, even the unbeliever couldn't deny that my God is a mighty God.

I didn't know why, but in one way, I was totally happy and surprised. But somehow, I also felt that I didn't deserve it or that I am unworthy to receive such a perfect love and perfect favor! But when I think about this scripture, "Simply because you are My child and I am your Heavenly Father. It's my desire to lavish My *love on you*" (1 John 3:1), that is a perfect special *word* to convince me to receive it graciously and joyfully. The ironic truth is that *there are no strings attached to God's love*—period! With these *words* in mind, I just want to obediently accept God's lavished love for me! As I mentioned earlier, timing-wise, this was about six months after I left Pastor Jim's house. I went straight home and told my mother that I could go to America.

Well, through it all, I finally, truly, completely finished the whole procedure. That means that I was sure that I could go to America. God knew that I thanked Him wholeheartedly, but I also had in mind that I wanted to give some money as a token of my deep appreciation to our Lord. I didn't know why I had that in mind, but I wanted to give 500 Taiwanese dollars (back then, that was about 12.5 US dollars). Although it didn't seem much, but that was all I had. In reality, there was a problem: I also had in mind that there were two things that I thought I must buy before I went to America. This issue was really a big conflict to me. As a matter of fact, I knew for a fact that when I went to America, I would have to work because we needed the money, not only for our sake but also for helping and supporting my husband's parents' living expenses as well.

I am talking about working, but in reality, I had concern about my head. In Taiwan, I had been going to a beauty salon all the time, and the labor was pretty affordable, so I went to hair salon weekly. But in the US, I didn't know how to fix my hair, so what am I going to do? The solution was to buy a wig to cover my head. I thought that was the perfect way to solve my hair problem. This meant that I really needed to buy a wig. In other words, the wig was a must-buy item.

There was another thing that's an interesting item to buy that was not exactly an important thing I needed. But I really didn't know why I insisted that I had to buy it. Why and what's the purpose? To be honest, I didn't have an answer for the question, and even to this day, I still don't know why, but I simply loved it and wanted to have it before going to America, so these two items I thought were very important things I must buy.

Money-wise, in reality, this was the big conflict because I wanted to give the $500 contribution to the church as my appreciation gift to God. That means that I couldn't buy those two items because the money I had, I could only either give to the church and give up the things I wanted to buy or buy the two items that I really would have loved to have. God knew that I really needed and loved to have both things. Well, this was a big stress and headache to me. Time was running short, but here I was, and I still couldn't make up my mind.

I didn't know what to do so I just changed my mind back and forth just about daily.

Talking about praying, I did pray diligently, obediently too, but I was still hanging my head and couldn't come to a clear decision. Interestingly enough, there were times when I compromised and rationalized to myself. Well, God is a compassionate and all-loving, all-knowing God. He loves me anyway, and He will forgive me for buying those two things that I need now at this time for me, and the donation could wait. I will give the contribution some other time. I made up my mind for sure: I will do it.

But the other side of me, the Spirit-filled inner part of me, felt terribly guilty, very restless, and I had no peace in my heart at all. From my own experience, *peace* is always the easiest way to tell me and confirm to me that I am obeying God's way or not. On the other hand, there were times when I decided to give to the church, but the carnal side of me felt terribly sorry for me, and I had strong feelings of self-pity. The unsettled mixed feelings of this kind of emotional struggle still remained the same. To be honest, it was just about driving me crazy. Day and night, I was very miserable.

Time was running very short, so I had to make up my mind and decide what to do. That kind of stupid, carnal way of thinking, with both emotional and spiritual struggling, lasted for a while. Until about two weeks before I flew to the US, out of the blue, one midnight, I woke up, and I asked myself, *Why am I waking up now?*

Without a second thought, I told myself that I must make a clear decision right now. I knew very clearly that the unsettled issue was the reason that woke me up. This time, I knew I must do it. I seriously prayed, and this was what I prayed:

> Dear Father God, I am so sorry about my delaying decision. All I want now is not important despite any reason. I now make up my mind that I want to give my contribution to You with a cheerful heart and with my whole heart. No more changing and no regretting. Please forgive my little faith, my stubbornness, my self-pity,

and self-centered weaknesses. Thank You for
Your perfect love and Your perfect forgiveness.

When I prayed that, the tears automatically naturally flooded my face. That was a sweet tear, the tears of joy and victory. That was the evidence confirming that my decision was genuine and authentic from my heart. God saw my heart and accepted my true repentance and graciously, truly forgave my sins, my wrong behaviors. I finally realized that all the past few weeks' struggling, the undecided attitude to surrendering to do the right thing was wrong before God and displeased God until I was willing to confess to God and truly apologize to God.

After I sincerely, humbly expressed all of my wrong behaviors to Him and genuinely asked for His forgiveness, I finally felt so good, relieved, and peaceful in my heart. I knew and felt thoroughly that God totally forgave my misconduct, my weak faith. The scripture says it well: "When God forgives our sins, it's like how far the east is from the west" (Psalm 103:12, I paraphrased).

The following day was Sunday, and I cheerfully and graciously gave away the money to my church as a token of my deep and sincere appreciation to God. Ever since, I continually felt peace and had absolutely no regret at all. The Bible says that whenever we give, we must give with a cheerful heart (2 Corinthians 9:7). The reality is that after I gave 500 dollars to the church, there was only fifty dollars left for me, and that was all I had with me. The fifty-Taiwanese-dollar equivalent to US dollars was 1.25 dollars. But I still felt absolutely peaceful and secure to go to America with that amount.

It was about one week or so before I flew, and I made an effort to visit my aunt, my mother's younger sister, the only sister left. I went to her house, and I just wanted to say hello and goodbye to her.

While we were talking and casually chatting, I told her that all of the procedures were done, settled, and I was about ready to go to America. I stopped by to say goodbye to her. We were in her bedroom, and while we were talking, she walked to her daughter's bedroom, and she had to go through the bathroom (the place that was in between both bedrooms). They used the same bathroom, and while she was walking through the bathroom to her daughter's bedroom, all of a sudden, she called my name and told me that there were two wigs that were hanging in the bathroom. She said to me that I could pick and take one of them for myself. I was totally shocked and surprised and didn't say a word.

A few minutes later, she came back from her daughter's bedroom. She sat down on a small chair before the dresser. Only a few minutes later, she pointed to a beautiful white makeup suitcase right next to her sitting chair and said to me, "Oh, yeah, this suitcase was for you. I brought it back to Taiwan from Japan, and I meant it to be for you."

Again, this time was even more shocking. I had goose bumps, and my body moved backward against the wall behind me. And I was still silent without saying anything, not even the basic common thanks! She felt strange from my reactions toward these two things that she was giving to me. She totally misunderstood, and she was aware of my strange reactions and even explained to me that the makeup suitcase was brand-new and meant to be given to me. "Don't you like it?" (she didn't know a thing, not a clue at all).

Finally, my emotion and spirit kind of woke up and came back to reality, and I said something to her. "Oh, yes, thank you. Thank you very much. It's very pretty. I like it." This was not talking only about the things themselves. There was a very deep, miraculous, awesome meaning and message behind the things. But of course, she didn't have a clue or idea at all. I'm glad that just a few years ago, I had a chance to tell her this story and thank her. That God had used her kindness in this beautiful story. She lived to be 103 years old, and she was very blessed to live to that good old age. She passed away in October 2022.

A few days later, I went to visit my uncle, my mother's twin brother. For the same purpose, I stopped by his company, and he took me out to lunch. I told him the same story that everything was done and had come to pass, and I will soon be flying to America. As always, like a kind uncle, he asked me questions and said good things, such as encouraging and inspirational words to me. At last, he asked me, "Do you have money with you?"

I replied, "Yes." I didn't tell him the truth that all I had was fifty dollars because I didn't want him to worry or feel sorry for me. I also said that the ticket had already been paid, and I heard that there was plenty of food on the airplane. "Jacob will pick me up at the airport. In fact, I really don't need the money." That's exactly what I had said to him.

We paused for a few minutes, and he said to me, "Uncle wants to give you 200 US dollars."

I was totally shocked and absolutely surprised about the money, especially the amount, so I just wanted to make sure and curiously clarify with him again. "Did you mean 200 dollars in US money?"

He answered firmly, "Yes," and repeated it, "Yes, it's 200 US dollars."

Emotionally speaking, I was absolutely overwhelmed, surprised, and completely shocked, and I didn't know what to say besides giving a heartfelt thanks to him.

The focal point wasn't about the money itself. It's ultimately a special gift given from God through my uncle. Back then, that was a huge amount. The currency exchange rate was one US dollar equals forty Taiwanese dollars. Back then, 200 US dollars converted to 8,000 Taiwanese dollars. In Taiwan, we could buy a handsome Suzuki motorcycle at that time. Therefore, what I had originally was 1.25 dollars only, but at the time right before I came to America, it changed from 1.25 dollars to 200 dollars. Therefore, the answer to the title of this article "How God Brought Me to US with USD1.25: In Fact, Did I Really Come to US with USD1.25?" The answer was from 1.25 dollars, through God's mysterious calculation and special blessing, He multiplied it to 200 dollars. You do the math. That's how much I really had!

Through it all, I have been pondering and carefully thinking about the whole amazing scenario or story. If I briefly summarize the whole scenario from the very beginning to the very end, I would like to quote this scripture to express my simple heart and mind in the whole story: "Blessed are the pure in heart, for they shall see God" (Matthew 5:8). It is the pure in heart who see God. It's interesting that when I was trying to pick a scripture to use for the concluding thought, I didn't know why I just loved this particular one. It's the pure in heart who see God. I asked myself why this scripture stirred in my mind and kept dwelling in my heart. I have been praying through how that related with this article. I just knew I liked it very much.

At the same time, there was another scripture that came along with it: "Delight yourself in the Lord, and He will give you the desires of your heart" (Psalm 37:4) I felt that God kind of used this scripture to answer my question for me. Therefore, it's the will of God who put it in my inner being. According to the Oswald's devotional guide, purity is not innocence; it's more than that. Purity is the result of continued spiritual harmony with God. Bingo, that's it! With the meaning of this comment, I can see the picture much closer to this story.

There is a well-known saying: "Wisdom cries out to the simple men—dumb, unsophisticated, and naive common people." That sounds like it's talking to me. There were a lot of times that my trusting, naive character has gone too far, even to the point of "dumb". Sometimes, it's easy to be confused with the naive, simple trusting and purity. I am sure there is a fine line, but it may not be easy to distinguish between the two of them, especially for me.

When I think hard and deeply, I remember that the very beginning of the story was started from a pure heart and obedient attitude, without quite knowing what's going on ahead. At the very beginning, I wasn't planning to go to the US. But it was God's plan, so He then used His own ways or strategy. Step-by-step, He guided me to move forward. My part was the same, carnally speaking. It's kind of blindly following His guidance and directions, yet I had peace of mind to follow the plans even though I wasn't too sure what I was doing ahead. When all had come to pass, I knew for a fact that God was orchestrating every moment, situation, and every turning.

In regard to those surprising, amazing, and strange gifts—the wig and the makeup suitcase—in general, I think that those are not the common, normal gifts that people give away as gifts. The mystery that caused me to keep on being bewildered and pondering was how come my aunt knew that I needed them at that time she was living in Japan and came back to Taiwan about two to three months later? At that time, we were in different countries, Japan and Taiwan. We had not made any contact with each other at all.

Biblically speaking, in essence, the only answer is found from God's sovereign design and power to fulfil His own pleasure. "Our God is in heaven, he does whatever pleases him" (Psalm 115:3). Indeed, the whole story is proof of the remarkable works of the Holy Spirit, who was working in His perfect designs and His perfect timing. Likewise, with the extraspecial blessing from my uncle of 200 US dollars, it's absolutely under God's special divine blessing as well.

The Bible says, "Every good gift that you receive comes from above, from God's hand" (James 1:17b). Those were the two things that I cheerfully and sacrificially chose to give up. Amazingly, God, in His own unique way, blessed me and rewarded me in very remarkable and wonderful ways at the moments when I received those two surprise gifts.

As for the money, besides shocking me, I felt that God actually dropped them directly before me from the sky. I felt that I was undeserving to receive it, yet I got it for fact. It's totally surprising and amazing. As for the other two strange gifts, the wig and the makeup suitcase, I received them with different interesting mixed feelings. Although I knew for real that the makeup suitcase wasn't needed in the practical way for me, I didn't know why I simply loved to have it for no reason (to this day, that is still a mystery to me). As a matter for fact, I have kept it for about thirty years, and I still didn't use it but enjoyed to have it.

There was an extra episode about it. As a matter of fact, when I was working on my graduate program, we were told one day to bring something special and share with the class what that meant to us. I knew that it wasn't a Christian school, but I still took my courage and did it anyway. I boldly shared the true story. There was a Jewish lady who came to me and said to me that my story really touched her heart.

Yet God still gave it to me in His unique way. God knew also that in a real sense, it wasn't important to me at all. It was simply because I just loved it—period! However, from this particular small act, I felt that this great I AM *being*, the heavenly Father, just like the real earthly father figure, I felt that He was so real that I could feel God's tender heart and His exceptional loving-kindness, which so emotionally touched my feelings deeply. There is an insightful saying: "The most modest form of love is tenderness. It means and expresses the deep emotional concerns." That's well said and a great insight.

In other words, I have seen the deep motivation of God's heart and His special personal compassion to make me happy, and it was *His* desire to lavishly reward me with His special, *tender love* for me. God didn't care whether it's practical or not, yet He knew that I simply loved to have it. He still gave it to me in a very sweet and amazing way. Simply from this small thing and small act, I have sensed and felt deeply touched from my Lord's tenderhearted compassion, and His personal tender love caused me to feel that my emotional being was in line and connected with God's Spirit. It was the evidence of this scripture, "Blessed is the pure in heart, for they shall see God."

Indeed, it is the pure in heart who see God and shall richly receive blessings from Him. With this precious incident, I think I found the answer for myself. With a sincere heart, I thank *You, Lord.* I praise You and adore You deep down in my whole heart. Thank You, Lord. It's through Your miraculous works and rich blessing that You miraculously multiplied from 1.25 US dollars and increased it to 200 US dollars.

Dear Father God, thank You for Your faithfulness and promises. The whole episode turned out exactly as You said in the very beginning, "If the door God wants to shut, despite of any situations, it will remain shut. Likewise, if it's His will to open, He will open regardless" (Revelation 3:7b, I paraphrased). Indeed, it's *You* who put that particular scripture into Pastor Z's heart (Psalm 37:4): "Delight yourself in the Lord, He will put His desire into your heart." For ironic truth and fact, it is simply with *Your Word*, and Your power is evident.

I think that it may be very hard for people to understand what I have experienced with God's special attention, His tender love, and the intimate relationship through these encounters. To some people, you may have thought, *What's the big deal? What's so special about it?* Yet for me, it carries a deep emotional concern in special relationship between just God and me, and that's meant the world to me!

This strange act, may seem like a very small incident, or you might have said that it's only a coincidence. As for me, I see that God Himself especially planned and reserved it for me, a dumb, unsophisticated, naive simple sinner like me. Yet He cared so tenderly in His heart and made it work. Deep down in my heart, I felt that He loves and cares for me as a very *special child* to Him in His heart. That's why while I was trying to express and describe those small details of the process, I still felt deeply touched now from then. Though it was a long time ago, it is still vividly freshly in my heart, and that's why that I am writing with tears, and I am touched emotionally and spiritually as well. No words can express the feelings of my true inner appreciation, a sense of satisfaction, true joy, and sweet rest that virtually saturated my whole being.

Dear Abba, Father, thanks for Your *Word* and *Your faithful promises.* You alone deserve all the praises and all the glory!

# I Was Baptized by the Holy Spirit

Before I start my story, I want to share a brief introduction about the prior background of it. We were living in Skokie, Illinois. Skokie is in one of Chicago's suburb areas. Believe it or not, it's considered the world's largest village.

One Sunday afternoon, there was a program on television about a group of successful Christian businessmen testifying how they became Christian. One day, as I routinely watched the show, there was a man on the show who proclaimed, "I was baptized by the Holy Spirit!"

With a puzzling and questioning mind, I asked myself, "What does this mean?" He was sharing a powerful story about what had happened in his personal life. Honestly, I don't recall his story. Some of the mysterious details were similar to mine. Especially, there were a few theoretical and supernatural areas that were identical to mine. Therefore, I copied the title of his story as the title of my article. "I Was Baptized by the Holy Spirit."

When I first came to America, we were living in Chicago, Illinois. One night I, my husband, and a friend from the church we attended in Evanston, Illinois, went to a theater nearby. The movie was a Christian movie. I don't remember the title, but I remember that the film was a production of the Billy Graham Evangelistic Association. The content of the movie was talking about the story of a young man who was kicked out by his parents. Packing up all his belongings into his van, he went to see his girlfriend. The girlfriend was a very devoted Christian. The day he left home was the same day that Dr. Billy Graham had a big crusade in his hometown. He knew for sure that his girlfriend would be there.

The crusade was very crowded, and the young man parked his car in the huge parking lot. He didn't know where to look for her. He was sitting in his car, waiting to see her after the crusade had finished. In the meantime, he was listening to Dr. Graham's message through the speakers in the parking lot.

The main message of the story was focused on Dr. Billy Graham's preaching. In his preaching, he said, "You know that we are all sinners, but do you know how God punishes us as sinners?"

It was very strange and interesting. There were two single words, *punish* and *how*, which struck my heart in a very profound way. As a matter of fact, it convicted me. It was a very heavy weight. I couldn't explain it to you. I could only tell you what had happened from my experience. This was how I reacted to the word *punish*: for only a split second, I found my heart wide open, curious, and anxious to hear Dr. Graham's answers.

The word *punish,* to me, I thought since it's a negative word, it'd be something not good. It'd be mad or scolding us more likely fit its meaning. Therefore, in my mind, I was expecting to hear that God would do something harsh, severe to punish us. That's my pre-occupied mind from His word of *punishing*. Since we are sinners, we deserve to be punished as sinners anyway.

When Dr. Graham said in the movie, "We are all sinners. … God sent His only begotten Son Jesus Christ to die for us. … How does God punish us?" How come all of those messages in that particular moment moved me like they had never done before? It was 100 percent brand-new to me in my heart and mind. Why? I really had no clue at all. I couldn't explain it. Just from my life experience and my own personal studying of the sermons, I have heard that kind of fundamental message countless times before. But why at this particular time and even happened in a movie theater? It's simply too strange—there is no way to explain.

The second word, *how*. Dr. Graham answered his question of "how God punishes us as sinners." Again, my heart was anxiously awaiting his answer. His answer was totally opposite of what I had thought in my mind. He said that God sent His only begotten Son, Jesus Christ, to die on the cross for your sins and for my sins.

Again, it's the same strange feeling, the message that God has sent His only begotten Son to die for our sins. I didn't know why, but I felt deeply sad, with a heavy heart. It seemed there was a thorn that pricked my heart when I first heard of it. I could feel, for a fact, like a real thorn had pricked my heart and stayed in my heart. It made me feel uncomfortable. I even wanted to remove it from my heart physically. Afterward, I couldn't concentrate on the movie anymore, but I was continually bothered by that thorn that pricked my heart.

In my whole Christian life, I always knew and confessed that I am a sinner. I am saved only by the grace of God. I knew Jesus died for all mankind. I am not particularly good or bad. I am simply an ordinary sinner, just like one of them. I never have felt so deeply, so strongly that it narrows down only to me at that moment. The point is He died for me. He died for me! Over and over again, it kept on dwelling in my mind. I have never felt that kind of deep conviction straight to my heart. The amazing transformational thought of a brand-new message and a brand-new meaning and a brand-new perspective of this message: "He died for me!"

The movie moved on, and so did my mind. I followed the episode superficially but not in my heart because I couldn't focus on the theme anymore. My whole being was utterly bombarded by the thorn breaking my heart. It's very hard for me to imagine experiencing this new revelation. I couldn't even explain exactly my inner mind and thoughts. In the same way, I couldn't understand or explain *why* and *how* that happened. It was an absolute fact regardless from any point of view.

Even now, while I am working and thinking on this particular incident, I was describing the details and processing the event. All of those details are like viewing the movie freshly and vividly through my memory again. And then, I found my tears flowing down my face and feeling deeply touched my heart.

Afterward, I did feel the full deliverance, spiritually and emotionally refreshed and recharged again. In addition, the byproduct of the very first encounter, I have never felt so convicted of my sins ever before. It has given me a much deeper sense of worth in Christ alone. Thank You, Lord. You have changed and strengthened the view of my self-worth because You have chosen me, adopted me, and called me as Your precious child. That means the world to me—all because of the fact that "You died for me!" From now on, in spite of any circumstances, I know that I don't have to fight for my self-worth, and it's done and finished forever and ever.

No, I couldn't stop sharing this precious and wonderful encounter firsthand. It seems that the unforgettable, unique memory is still real and refreshes me today as back then, the focal point was not simply to share this true story in every detail. In fact, those two strange incidents are strange as the stories themselves. Regarding the question "Do you know how God punishes us?" Why suddenly, it became a brand-new thing to me. It's true, and the fact is that it was an absolutely brand-new message to me! But in reality, I have heard about it in my lifetime from the church sermons or preaching and my own lifetime study.

As with many unusual previous stories, this was just another miraculous true story. Even to this day, I am still puzzled and have no answers. I suppose maybe I won't have any answers in this lifetime, and I see the Lord in person. I remember a long time ago when I watched TV, a news reporter had an interview with Dr. Billy Graham. He had asked him a question. The question was, "You are not only a Christian but also a well-known evangelist, not only in the United States but also around the world. Do you have any questions that you do not understand?"

Without any hesitation, Dr. Graham answered with a firm and honest response, "Yes, I do! I have made a long list and will ask Him when I see Him in person."

I think that's when I'll have mine too!

After we went home, my husband asked me, "What did you think about the movie?"

I said to him, "How can it be that we are sinners, and God didn't punish us? On the contrary, He allowed His only begotten Son to die on the cross for us on behalf of our sins."

While I was talking, tears suddenly burst from my eyes, then I was weeping, crying out loud, and even sobbing uncontrollably for at least twenty minutes. During that crying, I felt deeply sorry at first, guilty for my sins and ashamed in the way that I have never thought before of in my whole life. I know I am a sinner, but the people in the whole world are sinners too, and I am just one of them. But at that time, I felt that I was the only one whom He had died for.

I really have never ever felt this before. I strongly felt that He died only for me personally. I couldn't express with any human words how I felt unworthy to receive his beautiful and perfect love. I kept on crying and talking to the Lord. I am a terrible sinner, so very sorry for my sins, and I asked Him why He died for me. I didn't deserve His love and His forgiveness, to die so brutally and shamefully on the cross for me. Those were the thoughts that penetrated and dwelt in my head, my mind, and my heart. In absolute fact, I never before felt so deeply, extremely convicted of my sins individually. There is no way to explain!

In short, through this encounter, I experienced its meaning in a much deeper way in my mind and my whole being. With His unique divine *love,* I especially felt terribly sorry about my sin. This was a very special personal relationship, which I had never experienced before. Whenever I thought about this incident, I always felt overwhelmed. God's mighty, and His deity is so much bigger and greater than I could have ever understood and imagined! I remember a pastor who had asked a question of his congregation, "Do your heart and soul really sense and experience Jesus's pain on the cross for you?"

I now can boldly and firmly answer, "Yes! I do praise the Lord for this special Blessing!"

What a precious and awesome experience to behold. In fact, in spite of any aspect, there is no way I can describe or measure that *love* and myth of God.

There is something interesting, also a mystery, that I must mention. During the sobbing and weeping, I felt very tired and exhausted both physically and emotionally. I told myself to stop it, but I knew I couldn't stop. I strongly felt that it was the Holy Spirit's deep conviction and special, dynamic power working inside of me. I just couldn't stop crying! All those thoughts fully saturated my whole being, running deep and powerfully within me. After all of my thoughts finally straightened out, the crying simply stopped. It stopped not by my will but stopped by itself. Even the timing was about the same. How interesting that the time the businessman cried, that's the same time happened to me. I was exhausted physically and emotionally, but in the spiritual realm, I felt very refreshed. I felt like a new person, a free person. My relationship with the Lord Jesus was transformed into a new and deeper relationship.

Remember, Christians are also sinners, just like non-Christians. We also get mad or angry, harbor grudges, and experience disappointments, depression, and anxiety as well. There was a particular scripture that has a special meaning to me. I memorized this scripture very well when I was in high school. I had attended an English Bible study in a local church in Yilan, Taiwan, my hometown.

I still remember that the pastor was a Canadian. This scripture has stuck in my mind ever since. Therefore, the verse: "This is how my heavenly father will treat each of you unless you forgive your brother from your heart" (Matthew 18:35). Dr. Charles R. Swindoll was the founder of the Insight for Living ministry and served as the fourth president of Dallas Theological Seminary. In fact, my attitude and actual action were also confirmed by this verse. Pastor Charles R. Swindoll has said in his teachings, "Unless you really understand, truly believe, and accept God's forgiveness by faith in your heart, you will have problems to forgive others." How true it is. In other words, without the help or work of the Holy Spirit, we can't do it on our own—period!

Therefore, who is God to you? The Almighty and the Creator of the whole universe is depending on how we view or see Him in our heart and our mind. There is a story about a schoolboy. When he was drawing something on his paper, the teacher asked him, "What are you drawing?"

The boy answered, "I'm drawing God."

The teacher said, "Nobody has ever seen God. How do you know what he looks like?"

The boy answered, "You will see when I finish my drawing."

Surely, I know we all have our ways of viewing God in our minds and heart, just like this little boy. As for me, the mystery of this experience has made a great transforming impact on me. I also remember this verse: "I am the God Almighty, is there anything too hard for me?" (Jeremiah 32:27). When my life was so beat-up by all kinds of challenges and I was overwhelmed or stuck in the bottom of a pit, this is always a powerful message that gives me strength and encouragement. In fact, true story, a few years ago. I was troubled deeply by something important, and I didn't know what to do, and there seemed to be no solutions. I was thinking about what I should do.

While I was walking around on my big dining table, my mind was in deep thinking and full of anxiety, anxiously thinking of a solution. After I thought I had already circled around my dining table for at least three for four times, I suddenly saw on the table that there was a booklet, which also opened on the page interestingly enough. The scripture that shows on the page was Jeremiah 32:27: "I am the God Almighty, is there anything too hard for me?"

Believe it or not, when I first glanced at this particular verse, my eyes suddenly lit up. It seems that this verse has shown as a light shown in a dark room. I told myself, "What's wrong with me? I am stressed out about my tiny problems, but in God's sight, those are nothing to Him."

Rethinking and meditating on this powerful word, I did sink down in my mind and thoughts firmly. I prayed and thanked Him for who He is and apologized for my little faith. How could I forget and distract my faith from the all-knowing, all-powerful, mighty God? Mysteriously, but absolutely, the all-day-long-stressful and anxious thoughts suddenly disappeared. My mind was replaced with total rest and peace for no reason, though I still didn't know what the answers were and saw no solutions. Yet I was amazed and pondered, *Why do I have the totally peaceful mind and heart?* Then I realized that it's the supernatural work of God. I think the moment when I glanced at that scripture: "I am the God of almighty, is anything too hard for me?" (Jeremiah 32:27).

Immediately that powerful scripture, through the Holy Spirit's conviction, opened my eyes and reminded me to have a total view of WHO is God to me. We know that the Holy Spirit is a revealer of truth. And the truth is the God who I believe is an omnipotent, omnipresent, omniscient, mighty God, and He is actually working on these practical aspects.

The key element for the initiation of my choice to forgive those two people was the moment when my heart was deeply touched by God's love most closely. Immediately, I thought about two people in my immediate surroundings whom I didn't like, just like the Bible story of the parable of the Unmerciful Servant" (Matthew 18:21–35).

> Then the master called the servant in. "You wicked servant," he said. "I cancelled all that debt of yours because you begged me to. Shouldn't you have had mercy on your fellow servant just as I had on you?"

At that moment, I felt that I was like that wicked, unmerciful servant when I didn't forgive my two friends. All I wanted to say was, "Thank You, Lord. It's Your Spirit and Your Word that humbled me in Your presence and discovered my deep grudges."

I remember in Tony Evans's book *How to Live a Spirit-Filled Life*, he said,

> When the spirit fills your heart, you don't act, talk, think, and behave in the sinful nature or unnatural way. Indeed God's ways are good, perfect, and always above my own.

Regarding the Holy Spirit, we know that evangelical Christians believe that triune being, the third person of the Trinity—God the Father, God the Son, and God the Holy Spirit. In Hebrew, the word for God is Elohim. God the Father is the prime mover. Just as their names are different so do the roles and characters function differently as well. But They are equally important and equally significant. They are coexistent, always working together, inseparable forever, and have perfect relationship with one another.

Jesus promised His disciples and said, "I will ask the father and he will give you another counselor to be with you forever, the Spirit of truth. The world cannot accept him… But you know him, for he lives with you and will be in you" (John 14:16–17). So the work of the Holy Spirit is teaching us about God's truth and everything about God's divine deity, and sovereignty. Therefore, without the Spirit's discernment, we cannot understand God and His awesome truth, and He will be with us forever (John 14:16). And the apostle Paul says that a person who does not have the Spirit does not belong to Christ (Romans 8:9).

The Moody Bible Institute describe, "The Holy Spirit is a Christian birth right." Believers received the Holy Spirit as soon as they believe and accept Jesus Christ as their personal Savior in their hearts. Like the Father and the Son, the Holy Spirit is a revealer of the truth. Jesus's ministry on earth also depends on the Holy Spirit. Likewise, we should all do the same.

Thank You, Lord, for sending us the gift of the Holy Spirit. Thank You, Lord Jesus. It's You who asked Your Father on our behalf to send us the Holy Spirit to be a helper, Comforter, and counselor. He teaches us all things and reminds us of everything. The most important is the Holy Spirit who is only helping us to understand who Jesus really is as 100 percent God, once for thirty-three years as 100 percent human being—to reconcile and restore the broken relationships between God and human beings. "For he made himself who knew no sin to be sin for us, that we might become the righteousness of God in him" (2 Corinthians 5:21).

Again, praises to the Holy Spirit. Without His discernment and His strength, we will never figure out in our human wisdom or scientific intelligence, which God has made provision to forgive our sins through the atonement of His Son. The focal point is that nothing can satisfy God's wrath toward mankind's sin but only the innocent "blood of Jesus" (John 14:16–26). I heard a story about a conversation between the three, Buddha, Allah, and Jesus. Buddha said, "I see the way to heaven."

Allah said, "I know the way to heaven."

And Jesus said, "I am the way and the truth and the light. No one comes to My Father, only through Me" (John 14:6).

Yet it seems that it's a very common problem to thoroughly comprehend the sound fundamental doctrine in our hearts and minds, especially in Asia's cultural background. Our main religion is Buddhism, and many other small gods. I am very blessed that I was born into a Christian family. My neighbors and my school friends knew that we were Christians. They called my grandpa names and even ridiculed him. He didn't seem to care. On the contrary, he even boldly, calmly preached to them and tell them that Jesus is truly the God, the only God in the universe.

As for me, my school friends did the same to me. They called me names frequently just because of being a Christian. Back then, at that age, I was a Bible-ignorant kid because I never had read the Bible. But I didn't know how to react to this kind of situation.

As a matter of fact, I still vividly remember that there were a couple of times when my own teacher even insulted the Jesus I believe in front of me. It hurt my feelings inside of me. I felt sad but afraid to talk back. I also told myself because she didn't know my Jesus, and that's why she put Him down. I think Jesus will forgive her. I was in second or third grade. Although at that young age, I reacted to those insults and ridicules with the same attitude like my grandpa; I wasn't mad either. Afterward, every time whenever I think about that incident, I always feel very honored, blessed, and privileged. On the contrary, I even felt honored for being ridiculed in my heart.

Afterward, when I knew this verse, Matthew 5:11, I was amazed that this incident has perfectly confirmed my reaction toward this particular incident. "Blessed are you when people insult you, persecute you and falsely say all kinds of evil against you because me" (Matthew 5:11), back then I never knew or heard this scripture until much later in my Christian life.

Although this incident has come to pass under a number of years ago, to this date, it is still a great mystery to me, and I don't know why it happened. Every time whenever I think about it, I always feel very honored, blessed, and privilege to experience this beautiful incident. Dr. Billy Graham once said, "No one can fully describe the total beauty of God's love. It cannot be seen or understood until you actually process it."

> He has made everything beautiful it's time. He has also said eternity in the hearts of men; yet they cannot fathom what God has done from the beginning to the end. (Ecclesiastes 3:11)

How true is that! What a blessing and joy that I can actually feel that God's Spirit was dwelling in my heart through this incident. I received Jesus Christ not only as my personal Savior, master of my actual life. In the meantime, He is the best, precious friend to me forever as well.

*Concluding thought*

Thank *You*, Father God, for the gift of the Holy Spirit. It's the Spirit who made the presence of God available to all who believe Him (John 16). How often we forget that we have open access to the presence of God. What an incredible privilege!

I remember that Billy Graham has said on his teaching that the total beauty of his life cannot be seen or understood until you experience it, until you actually possess it. Indeed, the brand-new lesson, a brand-new perspective of the profound true meaning of He died for me. It simply runs so rich and deep in my being ever since.

On the other hand, I have great concern and passion for those who are still confused about the true understanding of the Holy Spirit as one of the triune beings. However, indeed, the Bible says so, I am glad that I am so blessed and grateful that I actually experienced it first-hand myself. In other words, I have actually experienced the Holy Spirit personally in tangible ways.

It also triggers me to remember one of my favorite songs, "Through It All" by Andraé Crouch. I just want to quote a few parts of the whole song. Those words and the melody are remarkably touching my heart and soul. Just as I actually experienced the precious new meaning of "He died for me."

Through it all
Through it all
I have had many tears and sorrows
I have had questions for tomorrow
There have been times I didn't know right from wrong.
But in every situation, God gave me blessed consolation.
That my trials come only to make me strong.
Through it all
Through it all
I have learned to trust in Jesus.
I have learned to trust in God.
Through it all
Through it all
I have been lots of places
I have seen a lot of faces.
There have been times I felt so all alone
But in my lonely hours
Yes, those precious lonely hours
Jesus lets me know that I was His own.

Yes, this is the key element that was revealed to me while I was sobbing, weeping, so sorry and so remorseful. That was also exactly depicting what I felt deeply for His special mercy in that time. I strongly and truly felt deep within my heart that He actually died for me personally. In His Spirit, I have felt in tangible ways that Jesus actually told me gently and firmly that I was His own.

Thank You, Lord Jesus, for bringing me so near to You and reminding me what it's like to be in close relationship with You. I feel very warm, cozy, and secure and imagined that as I was held by Jesus's tender arms. How precious and blessed!

# The True Story of
# Another Adoption

Sons are a heritage from the Lord, children are a reward from God.

—Psalm 127:3 (NIV)

*July 28; 10:07 a.m.*

Children are the best gifts God has given to mankind. When we first moved to Riverside, California, we attended Riverside Free Methodist Church. There was a family with four children: one boy and three girls. I loved them and was pretty close with their children, especially the girls. I had the girls stay overnight in my house several times. Back then, I did not have a child yet.

One day, out of curiosity, I asked the mother of the four children, "How do you feel that the three of them are your own, and the one was adopted? Do you feel differently toward the adopted one than toward your own?" Again, it was simply out of my own curiosity to know how that would work or how she feels in her heart.

What she said to me was totally to my surprise and beyond my imagination. "Children are the best gifts from God in spite of how or where they come from." In other words, they are all given from God as a gift. They only come in different ways.

My first reaction was total awe! What an awesome, beautiful insight and perspective (I absolutely believe that is true, but it is only in my head). I don't know how other people think or feel. As for me, I accept and believe that it is a biblical truth as well. The fact is at the time, I just couldn't accept her saying in my heart and feeling emotionally.

Regardless, it is the same blessing from God. Obviously, the key point from her was, "There is no difference between the adopted child and your own child." It struck me pretty hard, and at that time, I couldn't totally believe and accept in my heart that it was true. The Bible says so, so of course I believe it, but I still could not genuinely believe in my feelings. Generally, when something is strange or not transparent in my personal Christian belief, I always like to ask myself why and what's wrong with me.

There are two key factors that strongly impacted and polluted my biblically based belief. First, I was born and grew up in a traditional non-Christian cultural environment. This had a significant impact on my Christian belief, which I was not aware of myself. We were surrounded by opposing beliefs and deep cultural practices in the background. We also live in a culture surrounded by other gods, including wealth, social prestige, power, etc. When this happened, I discovered that my Christian value system had been confused with a worldly viewpoint. It even conflicted with the Word of God. I had never realized that my Christian belief on this particular subject had been distorted until this moment.

I remembered this when we were in Chicago, Illinois. While Pastor McGrew was visiting us, I remember that he said the same idea about it. He said that we are all created from the same God— *one God*—and someday, we are going to the same God, so what's the difference between your child and my child.

That's absolutely true. The point is that I have never had a child of my own. Anyhow, as for me, like I had mentioned on the other article before, I used to think that I had a pretty strong and solid faith that wouldn't be easy to be persuaded or changed. I was wrong about the adoption issue. Now, in a way, I am happy because this new discovery seemed to point out my wrong thinking and misconception. I think that without any personal experience, it is hard to have an objective mind or accurate conception.

How true that plain old wisdom is: "Don't jump to conclusions or presumptions too soon." It sure is true in this respect, that although the head and the heart's physical distance may not even be one foot apart, sometimes they can be hundreds of miles away from each other.

I had been thinking that I am not that strong or tough of a Christian. If I am just an ordinary sinful Christian, then what's the real reason behind the issue? Since I already figured out why, I want to obey and surrender before God's value and truth. So I have determined and chosen to utterly, absolutely submit myself to Him and die to myself. As Jesus said, "I do not seek My own will but the will of the Father who sent me" (John 5:30). He did the same thing during His ministry on earth. He realized and fully acknowledged His mission on earth was to fulfill His Father's plan and purpose. Praise You and thank *You*, Jesus, for setting a perfect example for me to follow.

The adoption of my two adopted children all came to pass a long time ago. They are adults now. I can honestly and boldly agree with that mother's point of view in my heart and mind: there is no difference between biological children and adopted children. It is simply the biblical truth that children are all God's precious gifts to us. With hearing both Pastor McGrew's biblical viewpoint and the lady's first-person experience. Now the correct idea of adoption was more firmly embedded and accepted in my head, my mind, and firmly in my heart as well.

Since the day we adopted them, I have been so blessed and grateful, despite all circumstances (for better or worse). Just like the mother of the four children (her name is Edith) who loves them all the same in her heart, I have finally totally agreed with her remarkable insight because of my own firsthand experience. Even though we have had some difficult circumstances and relationships during our life journey, I have never regretted one minute in my heart since they came to my home. To be honest, I even surprised myself, especially during those hard stages of the teenage period. I kept the same heart and the same attitude: no regretting. I don't mean to brag or boast how strong my faith was. In reality, I really need to credit God's mighty power and strength. I know for sure that I couldn't make it through without His presence and strength.

The scripture is always so powerful and reliable. It says, "In time of my troubles, God is my ever-present help" (Psalm 46:1). His Word is always the source of my strength. His strength is always enough to match our days (Deuteronomy 33:25). Through it all, I give thanks to God that all has come to pass. It is all because His Spirit is at work inside of me. When I fail and miss the mark over and over again, I run to Him. Although my children are now adults, I still love them dearly despite any circumstances or how they react to me in our relationships. I can say with honesty and dignity in God's sight that my love for them is coming directly and genuinely from God's solid divine Word. I truly think that was the *key element*.

As a matter of a fact, it was ultimately under God's grand plan for them to be my children. While I am writing this article, I remember Pastor Jon Courson saying on one of his radio Bible studies that when you are encountering hard challenges and you complain, blaming so and so, or saying it is someone's fault, you are blaming God. That was a very good practical message to confirm that I am on the right track in God's sight. That is something I would never want to do: to purposely disobey and question God's authority and deity. How they may treat me or react to me is not the most important issue. Rather, the most important thing is how strong my relationship with God is.

I have said it before and I want to say it again: in spite of any reasons or complex circumstances, my commitment is to God, and I will keep that commitment for the rest of my life. Even though it is beyond my understanding, my lifetime commitment is to love them from my heart, and I will stay firmly to my commitment until the Lord calls me home. In other words, the focal point is that I will love them regardless since both of them becoming my children is totally under God's grand plan and arrangement. Therefore, my commitment is first to God then to them. Because at the core of everything I do about the adoption of my two children, first and foremost, it has everything to do with my relationship with God!

I want to share an interesting story that happened on Father's Day. There was a young boy who received a letter on Father's Day. This was what the letter said:

> Like it or not, believe it or not, it is by the grace of God that I became your father, and you became my son. I didn't campaign for it, and you didn't vote for me either.

It's kind of interesting and humorous, but it also carries the biblical truth as well. It is by the grace of God that I became their mother, and they become my son and daughter.

> You may not know me; however, I know everything about you. (Psalms139:1)

> I brought you forth on the day you were born. (Psalms 71:6)

Indeed, those are the powerful *words* to confirm the adoption episodes.

My love and concern for them are very much the same as the way Christ loves me and accepts me unconditionally. It doesn't mean we have to agree or see things with the same view. It doesn't mean we will have a good relationship. It doesn't mean that I am bragging about how good a person I am and how devoted a Christian I am. All the reasons are beside the point. It is simply based on the truth that Jesus loves me and accepts me for who I am unconditionally.

The most important fact is that I live in God's will and plan and that they are my son and daughter. In spite of any circumstances, I love them dearly from my heart and will never stop loving them. This is my uncompromising attitude to obey God's grand plan for me and for them as well. Thank You, my Abba Father, for accepting me as I am and allowing me to be able to accept them as who they are.

Likewise, this is true between our relationships with our Lord, Jesus Christ, as well. In the end, regardless of our earthly relationships, the scripture says, "Simply because you are My child, and I am your Heavenly Father" (1 John 3:1). We are God's beloved children. I remember Pastor Jon Courson or Pastor Chuck Swindoll have said things like this: in God's sight, there is no such thing as "three generations." Grandparents or great-grandparents, we are all His children, only one generation—period!

I would like to share the brief details of the complicated adoption story. Quite frankly, it was a difficult and long process and journey in both adoption cases. Both were difficult but in different ways. In Naomi's case, the main problem was with US immigration laws, and in George's case, it was with Taiwan's government laws. In each case, there were about five or six different obstacles or problems that made it almost *impossible* to work out. It was really tough, and I didn't know where to ask for help or what to do. As always, the most effective way was to begin with the word *prayer!*

Regarding the *prayer*, quite a while ago, one of the lead teachers from the BSF (Bible Study Fellowship), has said to us, "Ladies, when you have any problems, go the throne, not the phone." We were laughing because it's a humorous way to say it, but it's true. It makes it easy for us to remember. Both adoptions were challenging, but they were under God's grand plan and His divine design. Because of His plan and His will, although it's hard and difficult, I didn't take it too hard or too stressful.

In George's case, he was born in Taiwan to a single mother. According to the Taiwanese government's regulations, all boys who are born in Taiwan are considered Taiwanese citizens. Any young man who is older than eighteen years old is required to serve in the military to fulfill a citizen's responsibility. For that reason, his mother wanted him to leave the country before he was ten years old. Otherwise, he couldn't have left the country until he turned eighteen years old and joined the army service to fulfill his responsibility. Besides prayer, I had to ask people how to get started and what kinds of things or what specific papers or documents were required.

In reality, the very first problem began from his mother. It was hard for her to let him go. His mother was hesitant to let him be separated from her. It's very understandable; she didn't want her only child to be separated from her and especially for him to come to the United States, which is too far from Taiwan. Back then, it was too far away. It would have taken maybe longer than twenty-four hours to fly. Yet the bottom line was that for George's sake and his future, his mother chose to sacrifice herself and not to keep him for herself but chose to let him to go to the USA.

But she was still resisting and wanted to keep him with her due to their emotional bonding and relational attachment. This was a legitimate concern and obstacle to release him for adoption. All the family members and relatives highly encouraged her to let go of him for his future's sake. It was really a huge hang-up. Time was running short. If she waited until too close to the deadline of the regulations, he would never leave Taiwan until he fulfilled his obligation to serve in the military.

As always, I began with prayer. I prayed for her to be able to release her son, the only child she had. On the other hand, I prayed for my husband's heart and my heart to be prepared to accept the idea of the adoption. At that time, our daughter Naomi was already living with us at our home in Riverside. Again, I began to pray, first for his mother to be able to let go of him and secondly, for our emotional preparation to accept him to be part of our family.

There is a very powerful scripture that convicted me and burdened me in my heart: "If you love and care for the least brother in your surroundings on earth, you care for me" (Matthew 25:40, 45 I *paraphrased*). This scripture was the key element and main purpose that motivated me in the very beginning. I really think that's the scripture that God's desire prompted in my heart. Somehow, I knew that in my heart. This was what I prayed:

> Dear Father God, *You* already know what's going on in our lives now. It's a very hard decision for George's mother, and since it's Your idea, please help us to be prepared in any respect as his adoptive parents.

During the praying and waiting period, the Lord had been working on both parties. George's mother's heart seemed to gradually soften and the same with both my husband's heart and my heart as well. During these complicated procedures, I went back to Taiwan to do all the legal documents for the adoption. Every time I got stuck or faced problems or any challenges beyond what I could do, I prayed like this:

> Dear Lord, You know that I have been willing to do the very best I can or do whatever it takes to comply to the government's procedures to make it work. You know right now the problem I have is way beyond my ability. Please show me what to do. Open the door, or please intervene. Do something, my Lord. I trust that You can.

My confidence was based on this scripture: "God won't let us carry the burden more than we can bear, when that situation happens, He will always help us to find a way out" (1 Corinthians 10:13 NIV, I *paraphrased*). Believe it or not, I had not known this verse yet, but that was exactly what I had in my mind. Afterward, this scripture became one of my favorite scriptures.

How did I know it since I had not read this verse before? Strange, isn't it? I think that I have an answer for it, which is found in Psalm 47:3 (NIV): "Delight yourself in the Lord, and He will put His desire in your heart." That is simply amazing and so true. All I can say is, "Thank You, Lord. You created all things simply with Your words. One word from You is powerful evidence." Pastor Max Lucado has said that faith is the conviction to believe that God knows more than we do. That's absolutely true, and I am the living proof.

Regarding the legal adoption procedures, there was an interesting episode during the complex process. God miraculously helped me surpass every single step. Most of the legal adoption paperwork had to be done in Taiwan. There was one very small thing that I needed, but it was in the States, at my house in Riverside. Though it was a very small thing, it was an extremely important document, which meant if we lost it or we couldn't find it, then we couldn't continue the process. Thankfully, I knew exactly where it was. The problem was, I was in Taiwan, and my husband was at home in Riverside.

The reason that I want to point this out was that I understood him very well. Unless the thing he wanted was shown right in front of his face, he would say he couldn't find it, or he doesn't know where it is. I hadn't known that special document was that important and was a necessary paper until then. As for my husband, Jacob, it was going to be very hard for him to find it. Therefore, I got a headache and started to worry. Now what to do?

Again, the best formula is to pray about it. I started to think that I should do the best of my part. I was told from the Taipei City Hall that this was a very important document, which was required. I wasted no time and went to the post office. I bought a telegram and started to pray and write on the postcard in the post office.

That particular special document was located in an extremely messy room. The whole room was full of papers, magazines, junk, etc. I told myself that it would be a miracle if he could find it. Regardless, I wrote a telegram in the post office, trying very hard to write as many details as I could to remind him and to help him to find that important document. At the same time, I prayed,

> Father God, *You* and I know exactly where the paper is but not Jacob. He had *no* idea where to find it. I have done my very best to describe as many details as I can. Lord, now *You* have to take over because the rest is beyond my ability. Lord, *You* know that without that "specific paper," the whole deal will be ruined and canceled. Please help Jacob to find that important document we need. Thank You for *Your* divine intervention.

Likewise, the same idea as Ruth Bell Graham has said, "My job is to take of the possible and trust God with the impossible." Thank You, Lord, for being the LORD of the impossible.

After I mailed it, I thought that it would have taken him a month or longer to find the paper and for me to receive it. The waiting period was expected to be a month at the quickest. Back then, the normal first-class mail took at least ten days, two weeks, or even longer one way. But guess what. I was amazed when I got it. It was within two weeks! It was totally unexpected to receive it so quickly. Jacob even sent it by special express mail, which was not his style, and I didn't ask him to do it at all.

Obviously, the reason that I received that particular document much sooner than the normal time frame was strictly based on his extraordinary concerns and efforts. Because he usually liked to save money on everything, I never thought he would spend the extra money for the express mail even without my asking or begging him. I was grateful he did.

I really think that was the Holy Spirit's mighty strength convicting him in his heart. As I have mentioned before and have experienced a few times, when the Holy Spirit is working, you don't act, think, or behave the way you usually do. This is another evidence of God's faithfulness to prove and tell me that He is ultimately in charge of the impossible issue, and He completed the course by Himself.

There were another two unusual episodes or incidents that were remarkable as well in the processing. One day, I accidently found out when we were just beginning to work on the adoption. While I was organizing or sorting things in my living room, I saw a piece of paper fall out of Jacob's Bible onto the floor. It was a prayer list. There were several items on it, but praying for the adoption of George was number one on the list. I think that indicated his special concerns in his mind and heart.

There was another amazing incident that also happened in perfect timing during the process. One of the procedures was that they had to send a social worker from the government or our local city authority to come to interview at our house. Afterward, there was a service fee or the expense that we must pay in order to fulfill the adoption procedures. To be honest, that part of the process, we kind of forgot.

The point that I remember well was that the charge for the service was about $2,000 or so. Unfortunately, the fact was that Jacob had been lain off from his company for at least a couple of months during that time frame. We didn't have extra money to pay that fee. There was a time frame for us to pay when it came closer to the due day. We were just panicking, worrying, and we didn't know what to do. As always, I prayed again for the miracle for God's provision for that money.

We honestly kind of forgot about it, but I think God didn't. I believe that God has perfect memory at all time. Strangely enough, it came close to within a week. About a few days were left before due date. All of a sudden, out of the blue, from our mailbox, we were surprised to receive a check of $2,000 or $2,200 unexpectedly. What a coincidence! You think so? Not us! I should say that was God's perfect timing to answer to provide for our prayers.

The background story of the check of the $2,000 was maybe about two years prior to that time. There was some kind of money that the company should have paid Jacob, and for some reason, they didn't and forgot all about it. He had mentioned and asked the company to pay him, but it had been neglected or what. The fact was he had never received that money.

As for Jacob, he had completely forgotten about that money. Somehow, I think God saved it for this particular reason! What do you think? In fact, Jacob himself had completely forgotten about it. God, in His perfect timing, dropped it to us when we really needed it. Thank You, Lord, for the perfect provision at the perfect time!

God made no mistakes, and He orchestrated throughout the entire story. How true! It's so true that God will always finish what He has begun. "He who began a good work in you will carry it on to completion" (Philippians 1:6). Thank You, Lord, for Your faithful promise! Because of Your sovereignty, You engineered it all along the way to make it possible for George to come to our home. This is all credited to You, who supernaturally surpassed all of those impossible obstacles!

Here are my concluding thoughts. There is an insightful saying like this: "Success is seen during the details of the process and the procedures itself." I totally agree. Although all of those detailed processes seemed like small or unimportant issues. The point was we couldn't have gone through the whole process without them, without every single detail.

We can't always see how God is working in His mighty ways. In general, I have seen lots of people, Christians as well, who mistakenly like to only see the results. There are lots of people who see God's way and only focus on the ending of the process, the results of successful achievements, and the performance on the surface. But the vitally important key elements are in the actual process and in the details of the procedures. It's in the midst of those hidden, seen, or unseen struggles—the small or big issues—that we can see how the mighty God, in His miraculous, amazing ways, breaks through, working out in His own unique ways what He wants to fulfill with His own plans. That's exactly what happened at the beginning of my prayers of this story. It truly confirmed the scripture of Matthew 25:40 and 45.

I can think of the "details issue" from a biblical perspective in the story in Leviticus chapter 9. This description of the sacrifices is studied by Jewish scholars at great length *because* it's the only time the procedure of a sacrifice is seen. Why does the Lord go into such detail? Why does He take virtually an entire chapter to describe this procedure? *Because* He cares about the details of how He is to be worshiped, just as He cares about the details and how we are to live. Our God is a God of incredible order. Likewise, He cares greatly about the details of your life and the details of my life and our daily activities as well.

One day, a lady approached G. Campbell Morgan with a particular question: "Why don't you ask the Lord about that?" he asked.

She replied, "Oh, it's too small a detail for the Lord."

"Tell me, madam," he countered, "what in your life is big to the Lord?" G. Campbell Morgan was right (from *Jon Courson's Application Commentary*). Because nothing is too big to God, the same is true that nothing is too small for Him either. As a matter of fact, quite a while ago, I had the honor and privilege and was asked to teach and conduct a workshop in CES (China Evangelical Seminary) in Taipei, Taiwan. In the midst of our class discussion about an important issue, someone had a question for me and needed to know the answer. Honestly, I forgot what the question was, but I remember vividly what I answered in the class. I said, "I don't have the answer either, but I do know who does. It is a very controversial topic and difficult to answer. But we should ask the Lord our God, regardless. I am sure He has an answer. We just need to pray to Him and ask Him what we should do and think."

There was another lady who gave an answer to the question. This was what she said:

> This was too small a question for God to answer
> us. God is a big God. He wouldn't care about
> such a small thing for us. Besides, God is too
> busy to care about such a small issue.

Unfortunately, in reality, lots of Christians are thinking that way in my surroundings.

It's sad to say that in our real world, we act with that kind of attitude, but it's very true, so true that even in our Christian lifestyle, we carry on this kind of misconception in our mind and thoughts at all times. It seems that it's commonly misunderstood by lots of people and Christians as well. That's why I try to describe the very details of the process to testify and prove that He is actually involved throughout the entire story and especially in the midst of the whole journey.

As for me, the most important I concern is that I have to tell the story exactly how it had happened, including the unimportant and insignificant issues during the process. Spiritually speaking, I feel that I am obligated to be a faithful servant by describing as much as possible according to God's instruction and guidance. From time to time, I have to keep on telling myself that I am writing all these stories because I was ultimately prompted by His calling and His plan, not to please people or for other purposes but for only one purpose: to obediently and faithfully write down what was based on the Holy Spirit's conviction, guidance, and revelation.

Likewise, I have exactly the same purpose and the same motivation for writing the two stories of both adoption issues. I am proud and happy to share both miraculous and beautiful stories with family and friends, especially those who are in Christ. This particular story is only telling about this bright, handsome young boy's becoming our son and the process of coming to the US. Regardless, the whole stories for both were quite different. However, in God's eyes, there are all precious and are beloved children in God's heart.

> You may not know Me, however, I know everything about you. (Psalm 139:1)

> I knew you before you were formed in your mother's womb. (Jeremiah 1:4–5)

> I determined the exact time of your birth and where you would live. (Acts 17:26)

Before I conclude this article, I'd like to share a few special stories about my two precious God-given children. Procedure-wise, Naomi came first. She was about four and a half year old and about four years younger than George. She went to school as a preschooler. George came to join us about five, six years later. He was about ten years old and was straight to fifth grade. They both have something in common: they are exceptionally intelligent, very smart children. They loved Jesus very dearly even when they were very young. The following are a few special memorable stories of them when they were young kids.

When they were young kids, they loved the Lord Jesus very much. They attended church Sunday schools and their youth activities just about regularly. They both loved to go to Awana and had a good time and enjoyed their programs. They both have had a strong belief in Jesus as their personal Savior and a good relationships with the Lord, Jesus. They maybe didn't know much about the scriptures in the Bible, but their relationships with Jesus were pure, simple, and strong even at their young ages. Whenever they had problems in their lives, they first called upon Jesus and asked help from Him.

Likewise, it reminds me that when I was in BSF (Bible Study Fellowship), the teacher said to us, "Ladies, whenever you have problems, first go to the *throne*, not on the phone."

I thought that's very insightful, saying in a humorous way, and easy to remember. And the same thing, that's what they have been doing in their young lives. Why did I say that? I like to share with you a few true stories, then you can tell for yourself.

When Naomi was in the school bus on the way to school, the girl who was sitting next to her had said unkind words to her. She responded to her, "I think Jesus doesn't want you to say that to me. Jesus said we should be kind to each other" (she was only a preschool student at the time). Question: who's with her at the time?

After she came home, she told me what had happened, and I asked her, "What do you think about that girl? And how do you feel, bad or hurt?"

She said, "No, she isn't a nice girl. I just leave her alone, ignore her." She seemed to not only have had a good relationships with her Jesus, emotionally, she handled the encounter with a very mature and healthy attitude. Excellent job, little Naomi. Age-wise, you were so young, but spiritually and psychologically, you did a perfect response in Jesus's sight!

Later on, my neighbor Marsha asked her, "Naomi, how come you can give such a good answer?"

She said, "My mother taught me!" In reality, I wasn't there at all.

There was another incident that was an incredible story as well. When Naomi was only five, six years old, I took her to a dental appointment one day. Two, three hours later, when we were walking to the parking lot, I didn't know that I completely forgot where I parked my car. Walking back and forth in the parking lot a few times, I still couldn't find my car. All the sudden, Naomi said to me, "Mom, we should pray and ask God."

As for me, as her mother, I admitted that I felt embarrassed even ashamed of myself, I actually told a little girl to do something that I was afraid/embarrassed to do. So I said to her, "Naomi, that's very good idea, but since it's your idea, why don't you pray?" (I felt a little awkward to pray in the huge public parking lot. What a shameful mother I was!)

Without any hesitation, she said okay, and she put the juice cup away and even closed her two hands and started to pray sincerely, "Dear Jesus, You know that my mom couldn't find our car. You are high in the sky. You can see everything and see where is our car. Please show her to find our car so that we can go home. Thank You. In Jesus's name, amen."

Guess what! I didn't know that after we finished the prayers, I was randomly walking, heading on a direction blindly. I didn't know where was I going. In only a few minutes, all of a sudden, I saw my car right ahead on my right hand. On our way home, she patted my shoulder from the back seat and said to me, "Mom, remember, next time, if you don't remember anything, just pray, okay?"

I humbly said, "Okay, thanks for your reminding." I felt that I was her kid, and she's like a little mom to me. That's a good reminder to me. Even at that young age, she already had a good relationship with Jesus. I still freshly, vividly remember this beautiful, naive, pure attitude, and her innocent prayers. It seemed that this just happened not too long ago.

This was another excellent story that I got to share. It had happened while we were watching TV on the screen. We saw a few black girls. They were naked, skin and bones. She asked me, "Why are they that way? Are they sick?"

I told her that they are poor, no food to eat. They are asking for people to help them out. She said, "Can I help?"

"Of course you may," I said.

She asked me, "How much is enough? Can I give them ten dollars? Is that enough?"

"That's not enough, but in your age, that's lots of money to give. By the way, how are you going to get the ten dollars?"

"That's true," she said. She paused for a few minutes then said to me, "I have an idea. Whenever we go to shopping, you always bought toys for me. But next time, when that happens again, remind me, and I want to save that money not to buy toy. Instead, save that money for them."

I told her that was a brilliant idea, very thoughtful and generous of her.

About a month later, I happened to need to do shopping. As with most of the time, she liked to look at the toys, and it was the same at this time. She found a toy and asked me, "Mom, can I buy this toy?"

All of a sudden, I remembered what she had said before. "Naomi, remember that last time, you said you want to save money to help those poor kids to buy food?"

Immediately, she said, "Oh, that's right. I did, so I am not going to buy it. But you must make sure to send them the money for me."

I said to her that I will. She did look at the toy in her hands. After I reminded her, she put it down right away without any hesitation or feeling sorry for herself. That kind of self-controlled behavior totally amazed me. Afterward, I told her that's very nice of her. She said, "Buying food for them is more important than buying a toy for me." She's only a six-year-old but acting like a generous, mature Christian adult.

The following is George's story. There is an interesting true story that happened before he came to the US. When George was before ten years old, there was an incident that happened in Taiwan. One day, my folks, my family, just decided to go to a fancy seafood restaurant for dinner, which is located in the outskirts of Taipei City. We had to walk through a big graveyard area, and that's at night. To be honest, even I felt very spooked and scared. George was walking with his uncle and one of the aunts.

During the walk, he's scared to death, even with his two hands circled around his aunt's and uncle's arms. However, he's still scared and frightened. Out of that very scary moments, he called upon Jesus and said, "Jesus, please help me. I am so scared. Please protect me. Please help me not to be so scared!"

The message of that simple, naive prayers and acts is telling me that to him at that superscary moment, only Jesus is his highest, the greatest and the most powerful authority figure deep down in his heart and mind. In essence, with his two hands already held tightly with his uncle and aunt, he should have told them that he's still very scared, but rather, he prayed to God and asked protection from his Jesus, the greatest and most powerful being in his heart. The message behind his act: I can see that in his hart, he truly acknowledged that Jesus is the only Lord of lords, and he trusted that Jesus's all-powerful being could really help him in times of his troubles.

This was a story to testify that he had a good relationship with Jesus since back then. I heard that before he came to the USA, when he was a young kid, he had gone to a church, and both the pastor and his wife were very kind and nice to him, especially the wife, who's also our very dear neighbor and friend. George's biological mother was also very nice and had been a very strong, devoted Christian in her whole life since she was a child. She had been compassionate, concerned very much for her son's belief in Jesus, and she built a good relationships with Jesus. I really think that couple, both the pastor and his wife, played a great, crucial role for George's and his mom's solid Christian foundation in their lives.

George came to join us at ten years old, no bedtime stories, but just about every single day, he always called me to pray with him before he sleeps. He even knelt down before the bed when he prayed. I wish I could have stayed longer with him. I regret that I wasn't able to do so!

There was a very special story I remember when he was about fourteen or fifteen years old. I don't remember what had happened. All I remember is that he stayed a couple of days in his classmate's house, who lived close to our house. It also happened around Mother's Day weekend. I was surprised that though he was not home, he still gave me a Mother's Day card. This is what he wrote on the card: "Although that I am mad at you now, but still want to tell you Happy Mother's Day! I love you."

I was totally shocked and touched deeply for his extra kindness and thoughtfulness. As he said even though he was mad at me, he still did that kind of act. That's a very deep, mature thought and behavior.

There was another profound story. I remember that one night, it was about midnight in the summertime, I was watering the front yard. Out of the blue, I was surprised that he just stopped by. I was very tired and was going to tell him to go home. But I thought he seldom came home, so we sat in the front porch, just enjoying the casual chat. In our talk, he shared with me about his business. He is really very smart, without any other help, no money, and no experiences, yet he still made good money. I thought he was a genius.

He said to me, "Mom, I want to tell you that right now, I don't mean to brag about that I am rich, but at least now in my life, I can pretty much buy or get the things I want to. But I truly realized that my heart was still feeling empty, and I know that emptiness isn't something I can fill but *only can be filled by the love of God.*"

My goodness, that's great insight. I was totally surprised for that kind of deep sharing and his firsthand discovery by himself. He figured it out from his own personal life journey through the marketplaces, in the business world, and his surroundings. He was about twenty-five years old.

There is a saying I quoted before, "Who is the best teacher?" The answer is your own experience. Great insight! I was very impressed and proud of you. Excellent finding, George. I think that God's pleased as well!

In essence, in their teenage periods, one thing I felt guilty of was that I didn't spent enough time for them or with them. They both had their activities. George is good at sports. He loved volleyball and was good at it. Naomi joined the school band and enjoyed playing flute in different occasions. It was during that crucial teenage period that I got divorced. Our lives were like hell to me and my children. After I became a single mother, I had to take care all of the responsibilities and obligations. To survive for fulfilling or maintaining the basic needs in our daily life. It was very stressful and difficult to me, especially financially (e.g., the basic house payment, the urgent bills, etc.). In reality, those challenges were extremely hard on me. Oftentimes, except crying and praying, I didn't know what to do! All my concentration was mostly on working hard to get enough money so that we could keep the house. I confess that I often took my anger and frustrations out on them, and as for emotional aspects, I was already in bad shape myself. I'd say that the three of us all got hurt and felt sad and angry at the same time in different ways.

They really had been neglected most of the time. Especially in their teens, during those critical ages. Those challenges were more than I could bear. In the very tough times, I often took my frustrations out on them. I seldom stepped in their lives, especially in the emotional aspect. That's pretty bad and hurt them as well. I admitted that I have neglected their emotional needs and others. I felt bad and regretted forever. The only thing I can do is apologize to them and ask for their understanding and forgiveness. As for me, instead of dwelling on my past failure of not being able to do more for them, in essence, the failure motivated me and drove me into the arms of Christ, to rely upon Christ's forgiveness and help.

It's true that teenage stage or period is hard and difficult in general. In the meantime, I wasn't being a good mother available for them. In reality, if we hadn't kept on trusting our Lord daily, it would have been unbearable. The good news is that we have our mighty God's special care and His special provision. We couldn't have survived.

There was a pastor; his name was Ray Ortlund on the Haven of Rest radio ministry. One time, he said on his teaching, "God's provision may be seldom early but never too late." That was a perfect teaching at the perfect time to minister to me. It's become my lifetime "powerful golden rules." Back then, I had been struggling with the money issue just about monthly, sometimes even daily. Therefore, that message had become my lifetime powerful belief and encouragement. That golden rule does not only apply on the money issue, it's also good to practice in any other issues as well. In regard to those mistakes I have done to them, I understand that nothing can make up for it. All I can say to them is that I am very sorry for what had happened during those hard times, and I sincerely ask for their forgiveness.

As their mother, regardless, we cannot reverse the past. The only healthy and happy way is with God's help to let go of the past in God's hand. Likewise, only with God's supernatural strength, they will still be able to enjoy the good life ahead for the rest of their lives. I know firsthand in my life that's just true and fact! My whole life, I had been neglected since my childhood and also in my married life as well. The complicated impact from all of those encounters of the inner pains, heartbroken anger, etc. were unbearable without constantly, continually, persistently crying out to Him, clinging to Him. I shouldn't be still alive by now.

I will never forget there was a very special, precious moment, maybe a few years after I got divorced. One day, I didn't know why I suddenly felt extremely sad and feeling empty and feeling that nothing's important in my life. Life was nothing to me but only emptiness, and I felt that I was the only one alive in the world.

Suddenly, there was a saying that came to my mind: *You don't know God alone is enough for you until you have been there.* Previously, I didn't understand what that meant, but at that particular special moment, I truly and actually understood and realized what it really means. Indeed, at that precious moment, I deeply felt that God alone is enough for me. Then I sang the song myself in tears and felt comfort, soothing, and sweet peace in my heart and soul. "Trust and obey, for there is no other way to be happy in Jesus. Trust and obey." I sang it repeatedly over and over again with tears of joy, and I really felt so deeply connected with the Spirit of God,

*Conclusion*

All of the remarkable and miraculous works through the adoption journey, God has proven His faithful provision and His promises in every step, each hang-up, or turning. He finally accomplished those difficult adoption processing and was able to bring our son, George to US and become our legal adoptive son. Likewise, with the same heart and attitude, I used the same scriptures to encourage our first adopted child, our daughter Naomi. The key element was based on what God says: "I determined the exact time of your birth and where you would live" (Acts 17:26).

In short, the journey of their adoption procedures and processing was very much different and challenging. They were all under

God's grand plan and guidance and direction and in His time frame and His unique ways as well.

Thank You, Father God, that it's *You* who has brought George to become our son and to live with us in America, the beautiful country. Praises to *You* alone, and I give glory to *You* alone as well. May George, his biological mother, and I appreciate *You* in our hearts for the rest of our lives. We prayed, and God opened the door and fully accomplished His masterwork in His ways and in His timing!

# Completely Surrender before God, Part 1
# The First and Foremost Important Lesson in My Life

My purpose will stand.

—Isaiah 46:11

That he who began a good work in you
will carry it on to completion.

—Philippians 1:6

Delight yourself in the Lord, He will put His desire in your heart.

—Psalm 37:4

The God who made us knows us the best, even more than we understand ourselves. In His grand plan, everyone has been chosen by our Lord to serve Him in different ways for His pleasure and glory. When God wants to do a project, He will do whatever He wants to accomplish His goal (Philippians 1:6). We understand that God has His own unique way to shape us, mold us, and discipline us. If we keep on following His guidance and direction, in the end, He will help to accomplish whatever He has prepared for you. Be sensitive and be willing to surrender completely to His divine conviction. This verse confirms His absolute sovereignty and authority:

> From the beginning, from the ancient time…I say, "My purpose will stand, and I will do all that I please. … What I have said, that will I bring about; what I have planned, that will I do." (Isaiah 46:11)

In my whole life, I have never thought about surrendering to God, only sometimes. The God who made me for who I am, knows me well, and He uses His own way to guide me and to convict me in my daily life. The following story is the way He opened the door for me to learn His lessons thoroughly and deeply in His ways. Here is the true story of the details of my learning journey of this particular lesson: *completely surrender before God.*

In 1970, I came to Chicago, Illinois, to join my husband, Jacob (from Taiwan). Two or three years later, we started going to Hillside Free Methodist Church in Evanston, Illinois, which was only a few miles away from our house. I would say that the church was the best church I have ever attended in my life. The teaching was excellent, sound, and very practical. I was not only receiving sound teaching but also enjoying the small-group fellowship as well. In other words, we both enjoyed and benefited from the teaching and fellowship with the congregation very much.

We joined that church after about three or four months. One day, out of the blue, Pastor McGrew stopped by our house for a social visit. We had a very good time getting acquainted with each other. Right before he was going to leave our home, all of a sudden, he asked us, "Is there something that you want me to pray for?"

To my total surprise, I answered immediately without any thought or hesitation, "Oh, yes. We have been married for a few years and have been praying to have a child." I used a complaining tone and demanding attitude. I also asked him, "Why have I been praying so hard for a long time and God still didn't answer my question?"

Pastor McGrew came back to sit on his chair. "I am very interested in your question." He said to me, "Yolanda, I understand how you feel. In general, when we pray to God and don't receive the answer from Him, then we get mad at Him.

"To God, we are like little children. If we don't get what we want, then we are mad at Him. As a matter of fact, we have had a similar experience like yours. In about the first three years or so, before we had our first child, my wife used to pray with that kind of attitude too, praying frequently and asking God to give us a child. The same prayers repeated all the time, and she was disappointed and mad at God too."

Therefore, he talked to his wife about it. This was what he said to his wife: "I understand that you have been praying for a child for a while and was disappointed that we haven't had the child yet. But I want to encourage you the same that instead of praying for a child, as a Christian, that the first and the foremost desire and attitude you should be praying is how to *completely surrender before God* rather than simply praying for a child regularly. It seemed to me that you are telling God to do what you want Him to do for you, and when He doesn't answer your prayers, then you get mad."

He was honestly sharing the experience of their true story with us. I didn't know why. Immediately, I totally opened my heart and told him that I had been acting exactly the same way. He said to me, "Yolanda, I understand we are all human and have a sinful nature. We all want what we want, just like the little children."

I want to pause here to point out some interesting background behind our conversation. There are a few things that I want to point out. First, before Pastor McGrew's visit, regarding the strong desire of wanting and longing for a child, which was secretly in my heart, there was no other living soul who knew my secret. It was only between God and me. It is so easy to stay in the depths of sadness and self-pity.

Second, gradually, I had to confess and admit that I had been suffering with a deep depression, and no one knew. I didn't know why, but on this particular moment, I suddenly spoke up without any hesitation. The secret of longing for a child in my heart, I just couldn't talk to anyone. But why, at that moment, was it suddenly coming out from my mouth so naturally?

That inner pain and sadness eventually caused me to suffer a depression that I didn't even know. All I knew was that I had been crying a lot without telling anyone. The unusual immediate response to Pastor McGrew's question was totally shocking to me, and I didn't understand either. It is simply amazing and strange to me. I only knew that it came out from my mouth so quickly and so easily without any hesitation.

Regarding this matter, I have been thinking and pondering about it for a while. But why? The only reason that I could explain is that it was the Holy Spirit empowering me to obey all that Pastor McGrew shared at that moment. Indeed, the power of the Holy Spirit was actually at work in me, nudging and controlling my heart and mouth. Besides, Pastor McGrew wasn't someone who was very close to us at the time. We had only known each other for two or three months. Therefore, the incident of Pastor McGrew's stopping by was not a coincidence.

The Bible says, "Do not worry about how you will defend yourself or what you will say, for the Holy Spirit will teach you at that time what you should say" (Luke 12:11–13 NIV). I think that was exactly what had happened in this situation.

Third, in addition, there was another wonderful incident that happened. At the end of that very same night, before I went to bed, I don't know why all of a sudden, without thinking, I just knelt down before my bed and started to pray, and I found myself praying out loud and crying so sadly and remorsefully, "Dear Father God, I am so very sorry about my ignorance and my wrong attitude toward You so stubbornly for so long. But today, from now on, I don't want to pray for a child anymore. Father God, I really don't want anything. I now know and truly realize that to have a child is not the most important thing for me in my life but to learn how to *completely surrender before you!*"

It was a powerful moment. Thank God for this precious and unprecedented moment in my life. That was a decision I experienced in Christ: *the freedom I chose to obey!* Unbelievable! That's a very heavy weight. Heartfelt words simply, surprisingly came out from my mouth. In short, the detailed process stories have been remarkably amazing and beautiful, which I could hardly express with logical human reasons. It made me ponder and pay attention to think it through, that it was absolutely, mysteriously engaged with God's design plan.

Obviously, for me, the focal point for Pastor McGrew's visit was God's plan because the feeling of the strong desire of longing was dramatically changed suddenly. Even I was surprised that I was able to accept it so easily and quickly, both emotionally and spiritually. In fact, the heart of the determination was fully and genuinely to accept the importance of learning this particular brand-new lesson in my life: *totally obeying whatever His plan for me in the future to come.* It's simply a miracle.

I felt so relieved, refreshed, and peaceful. That desperate feeling of longing for a child ran so deep. But now, that emotional feeling completely disappeared! The longing for a child finally had come to pass. The freedom from the daily haunting, like a shadow from my inside brought by the Spirit, was palpable. Emotionally speaking, I couldn't stop asking myself this question: "How can that be?" Something that was impossible to give up—how could I just give it up within one day so easily and so cheerfully? The long battle with the deep pains and shame, struggling to stop, despite my begging God in my prayers—why have those mixed feelings suddenly mysteriously disappeared?

To be honest, I want to confess that while I was writing about this, I still felt sorry and self-pity for those awful inner sufferings from back then. However, I think that the residue of the pain and aching inside of me still brought tears. Maybe it will never go away, but it's okay to be in tears sometimes. The tears are mixed feelings of sadness and victory.

I simply could not stop praising Him. My heart prayed like this:

Dear God, You are worthy of all praise, all honor.
Your steadfast love to me is more than I could
ever imagine. I could never figure out with my

own mind, "Why did You do that for me?" I couldn't stop thinking of all the details of what had happened. I couldn't use any words to express my heartfelt thanks to You. After all, I am just unworthy to receive Your special mercy and tender love. All I did was simply surrender before You completely and totally. You did it all by Yourself.

The scripture says it well: "My counsel shall stand, and I will do all according to my pleasure" (Isaiah 46:9–10).

For a while, emotionally speaking, sometimes I still kept lingering and pondering this question in my heart and mind! "How can that be?" I asked myself. I remember that one of my favorite songs "You Are My King" by Newsboys, has a line: "How can that be?" It was His amazing love, just as this song says, "Amazing love, how can that be that you, my King, would die for me? Amazing Love, I know it's true. It's my joy to honor you in all I do. I honor you."

I don't know why every time I sing this song to myself or at church, it always touches my heart deeply, with tears flowing over on my face. My heart can't stop saying, *Thank You, Lord. You are simply awesome. I want to praise You from the bottom of my heart and soul.* The words and melody both make me feel very emotionally touched.

In regard to *surrendering completely before God*, in my Bible study with Pastor Jon Courson about Noah's story, there was a little section from his comment:

> Salvation begins with death. It begins when I say, "I am dying to self. I no longer DEMAND MY OWN WAY, but rather give myself completely to You."

What a message! The Lord was using this statement to remind me loudly and firmly because it was exactly depicting my situation, and it also reemphasized the importance of the fundamental truth of "demanding my own way."

Thanks to God, it finally has come to pass. It was absolutely by His perfect love and grace and through His spiritual strength at work in me. I finally came to realize, and willing to accept the lesson which I have learned, "completely surrender to God" with all my heart, which also means "DYING TO SELF." This is very serious matter in my young Christian journey, yet I'm still determined to accept it with a cheerful heart. I think it's a blessing to have this attitude and determination in my heart. I'd like to praise Him for His grace and supernatural strength working in me. All credit to Him alone! I know that I am a slow learner, and it has been a very long, painful journey. I think that only He knew that it must have taken this unique way for stubborn me to learn this particular lesson. Regardless how hard or crooked the road has been, it's absolutely worth it!

God helps me to not give up on the most important lesson in my life: *completely surrender before God.* The reward to me was a beautiful and wonderful deal! Father God, thank You for Your rich blessings, which are more than I could ever imagine or deserve.

# Completely Surrender before God, Part 2
# The Actual Procedures of How the Baby's Coming!

On the second day, I started to practice my brand-new lesson with a strong commitment. I remember Dr. Chuck Swindoll's teaching: "putting the truth into practice." I loved it when I first heard his Bible study teaching. I've studied his teaching from the radio, along with his study guide, for at least eight years. I loved Pastor Chuck's solid, in-depth teaching and his great sense of humor. I considered that my privilege, blessing, and honor. Ever since, "putting the truth into practice" has become my ultimate goal in my daily life. Because faith comes from hearing and hearing comes from the Word of God (Romans 10:17), faith is vital to our Christian walk.

I remember during Pastor McGrew's visit—besides learning this particular new lesson: *completely surrender before God*—after the second day of Pastor McGrew's visit, something was different. I couldn't tell exactly what it was, but I knew that I felt like a different person than before. My heart was full of the excitement with a new attitude learning this incredible lesson. I didn't know why, but I felt that there was a sense of urgency for me to practice my brand-new lesson of *surrendering completely before God*. I felt that in my regular activities, I was more focused on application. This has never happened before.

Gradually, I felt more at peace in my mind and thoughts than I used to be. I have to confess that I used to be very inconsistent in being submissive to Him. It was up and down, not steady. Gradually, I felt that my life was walking in the right direction regarding obedience to Him—not perfect but improving. I was happy and enjoying my new life.

About six months later, I felt that my peace of mind was more consistent and stabilized in my daily life. Our marital life was improving as well. We have had less conflicts in our relationships. I knew that it was a spiritual battle controlling my life. Somehow, down in my heart, I felt that I was doing fine and mistakenly assumed that it would last me for a lifetime and that it would be much stronger than before. Therefore, I have asked the question, "Now, dear God, what do You want me to do next?"

I thought that I was in good shape and ready to accept God's new assignment. I was excited and ready for His assignment. But in reality, not really. There was a very strange thought about the idea of *adoption*. My first reaction to the idea was strongly *no*, so I rejected it right away without giving it a second thought.

There is a story behind the *adoption* issue. Again, it happened during Pastor McGrew's visit. Besides sharing the idea of total submission to the Lord, he also said to us, "I know that God has a plan for each one of us. I don't know what His plan is for you. Suppose God doesn't give you a child of your own. Don't you think that there are lots of children who need parents?

"Likewise, some parents who don't have children of their own would love to have a family of their own. Why don't we just share our love for each other as a family?

"Besides, the truth is that we are all created by the one God, and someday, we will go to the same God, so what's the difference between your child and my child?"

That was exactly what he said. I still remember him saying that clearly, but it didn't mean anything to me then. Besides, I wasn't paying much attention either. At the same time, I was greatly impressed, and I admired his godly perspective. I felt embarrassed that I, a so-called Christian, never had that kind of biblical perspective. Both my husband and I have seen things differently but not on this particular issue. We were both on the same page. We didn't like the idea of adoption. Why? I suppose the main factor was impacted by our traditional cultural background. Even though we are so-called Christians, we still live under the influence of our traditional cultural misconception.

Now, regarding the idea of the adoption, I just didn't know why it started to hit my mind again. For the first few times, I rejected and pushed it away from my mind. In fact, the more I pushed it away, the more it came to bother me. I resented the idea. I told myself, "No way! Both of us don't like it, so forget it. No need to think about it. It's impossible for both of us to accept this issue."

Time went by, and my peaceful mind wasn't that peaceful anymore. This kind of inner struggle kept on changing back and forth in my mind for a while until my peace of mind was getting out of control. It meant that my heart started to lose my inner peace and sweet rest. I finally figured out that the idea of adoption was conviction by the Holy Spirit, so like it or not, someone has said that when it's a heart issue, we must face it.

Like I mentioned earlier, nothing is accidental to Christian life, but the carnal side of me naturally denied and avoided the Spirit's nudges. Regardless, we still didn't like the idea. The unstable emotional status lasted for a long time, and I had no idea what to do. Every time I refused to face it, I felt guilty. This kind of mood persistently swings back and forth.

Interestingly, as the pattern in my new Christian life, I should bring it to the Lord in prayer, but not on this issue. Why not? Yes, why not this issue? I simply couldn't make up my mind. I challenged myself with the same question: why not? Because what if I bring it to the Lord in prayer, and what if the Lord tells me I ought to do it, and I said no to Him? That will be very tough and hard. It would mean that I purposely disobeyed His calling or His plan for me. That I would intentionally disobey and challenge His authority would be awful. I didn't want to do that. Therefore, it caused me depression and anxiety. The resisting also indicated that I openly answered to the Lord, "No!" Remember what Pastor Swindoll has said: when God calls us, we can only answer to Him, "Yes, Lord!" Period.

I strongly challenged myself, "Didn't I just encounter and declare a victory of learning the surrendering-to-Him lesson recently?" Ever since, I thought it's been encouraging heading on the right path in God's sight. I was happy and thankful for my walking closely with the Lord. But now, why, when the idea of adoption has come up, my heart was getting more disturbed. I couldn't remain in peace and rest anymore. In effect, that avoiding and refusal couldn't help me solve the problem. In other words, the byproduct of my constant refusal was only leading me to be more miserable.

One day, I questioned and challenged myself, haven't I just learned a so-called brand-new precious lesson, "completely surrender before Him?". But what happened now? Ironically, the *only* way to deal with it was to face it, which meant to bring it to the Lord in prayer. I knew in my head that theoretically, I knew in the very beginning. But emotionally, I was still having problems surrendering to His will. From those details of the process of resenting about obeying completely to Him, I could see that I was still as weak as I had been before. It seemed that I had not learned the lesson at all. *How sad!*

Like the apostle Paul says, "For I do not understand my own actions. For I do not do what I want to do, but I do the very thing I hate" (Romans 7:15). During that confusing and bewildering moments, I have thought about Romans 7:15, which very much described my struggle through emotionally and spiritually unsteady situations. How true and sad! I then felt very disappointed and ashamed of myself.

I then put in biblical perspective that at any time, in any situation—especially in a crucial moments or when making decisions—if I forget or don't actually practice having a Spirit-filled heart and attitude to make my final decision, despite how pious I am or how strong my faith is, for sure, I'll easily to fall into the pattern of my carnal thoughts and ways. However, from this encounter I experienced firsthand, but still hard to believe, yet the fact was the evidence to prove that how I actually, totally failed. It's not what I thought or imagined. This scripture says it perfectly and powerfully: "Apart from me you can do nothing" (John 15:5). Again, thank You, Lord, for reminding me and strengthening my faith through this incident. Again, it's evident proof that the scripture is so perfect and true that anytime I depart from His word, I am still a very vulnerable sinner. As I sit in shame, puzzled over my sad reaction of the adoption issue, it's simply a shameful joke. The previous so-called victorious experiences were all empowered by the mighty work of the Holy Spirit. Without His help, I am nothing and couldn't do any good thing. I must recognize and meditate on that solid fundamental truth over and over again.

Another profound insight I saw clearly is that this incident was another true factor to remind me that carnally speaking, in every step or every turning point of my life, if I don't totally depend on His strength for help, my sinful nature and weakness will be the same, doing what my sinful human way wants. It reminded me of a song: "I need you every hour. Every hour I need you." How very true, so true! I must always carefully meditate and apply those words. It's so real and practical. The only way is to take care of it and deal with it.

Yes, now, it's time to put the brand-new lesson of adoption into practice. No longer cling to the old pattern and put it off or avoid it. I'd say that this is another huge lesson that was God's plan for us to learn and to act upon. Even though we didn't know what His plan was ahead. We can only follow His guidance and direction step-by-step by faith even without knowing what's going on ahead in the next step or future.

I remember Abraham's story. He simply followed God's leading without even knowing where he was going ahead on his journey. Indeed, that's a good biblical example and a good reminder, so finally, the stubborn me started to face it and became willing to act upon it. I believe that *prayer* is always a central and most significant part of any service and ministry. In so doing, I brought it to prayer. "Dear Lord, You have persuaded me to accept the adoption issue from 100-percent no to 100-percent yes!"

Unlike the first day of Pastor McGrew's visit, the three miracle issues have come together amazingly and wonderfully within one day. Unbelievable! But on this particular issue, it has taken almost a year for me to learn to overcome and finally, with a cheerful heart to accept it.

During the process of walking through it, I simply prayed without ceasing. I have also prayed like this:

> Dear Lord, You knew that deep down in my heart, I still wanted to have a child from us, but since I want to surrender completely before *You*, I want to sacrificially give up my desire and will take whatever You provide for us. If adoption is what You prepared for us and was Your way of giving us a child, I am willingly and totally accepting Your plan for us.

My heart continued to pray like this:

> Lord, thank You for changing my heart to Your ways. You persuaded my heart just like a ball that gradually, slowly turns to Your direction as You have prepared it in the very beginning.

Amazingly, I actually felt it in my heart during the process of turning and pursuing the journey. "In the end, I am still utterly surprised how You, Lord, had changed the stubborn me from no to yes. I couldn't explain why but knew for a fact He did it all His way and in His time frame.

Now, I was fully ready and totally convinced to accept the adoption issue myself. As for my husband, I understood well and predicted how he was going to react, but I must try. One day, I approached him and asked him, "What do you think about the adoption idea?"

He answered, "No, I don't think so. I don't like that idea."

It was my prediction, not surprising at all. As for me, I reacted calmly and with a quiet spirit. To be honest, that wasn't normal for me either. Most likely, I would be mad, disappointed, and try to say something to persuade him, but not this time. First, I was silent for a few minutes. I only gently reminded him and questioned him. "How about we recently just have learned the lesson of completely surrender to God? What do you think that in this case, it is God's way to provide for us a child? Are you going to say no to Him or submit to His will?"

Silence—no answer.

I asked again, "What do you think that we just begin with prayer for this special adoption issue. No need to hurry to decide but simply to pray and ask for God's guidance and direction."

Silence. I think that meant no objection. I was just guessing. I understood that he's debating and struggling with surrendering and wrestling in his heart.

During the uneasy and confusing waiting period, I simply prayed silently, prayed for him, and prayed for myself for the wisdom not to push him to make a decision. I thank the Spirit's strength and discernment. I didn't rush him to make the decision. Somehow, I reacted calmly and patiently. I didn't know why, but I knew for a fact that it was God who was working in his heart.

I noticed that he seemed to be acting unusually quiet. I could tell that he has been seriously thinking, searching for God's will in his heart. Getting to the point, it was about two or three months later I did ask him again, what does he think? He still answered no, but the attitude of the rejection was softer than the first time. As for me, the same attitude. I didn't want to rush him but simply kept on praying for him with the hope in God's hand.

Our daily life went on quietly, slowly for a while. I checked with him every two to three months at least three times. The last time, when I asked him, he finally said, "I think it's okay, but I am afraid that someday if we have our own child after adoption, I will treat the adopted child differently, and that's no good, not fair to the adopted child either."

I said to him that he won't do that; it won't happen. I told him that he will love them the same. He knew that doctors have never said that we couldn't have a child. It's just a mystery that we couldn't have a child of our own.

It's very interesting the way God worked it out. At first, He worked on me until I was convinced totally. Then He started to work on my husband and had me as His assistant to stand by his side, helping him walk through to the end. He first worked individually and separately one at a time. "Father God, You are simply amazing and awesome. You deserve my worship wholeheartedly."

Well, the work of convincing or nudging us to accept His plan of adoption finally seemed to have gone well. The result of His plan seemed to have a happy ending. Both of us by now were totally convinced and persuaded by God in His way. As a result, God always has His own unique way to achieve what He wants to accomplish despite how difficult or complicated that journey is.

I prayed and asked the Lord for the next step. At first, we thanked Him and praised Him for the process of all the details. Finally, both of us were accepting the issue of adoption wholeheartedly. That's the sign to indicate that we were heading on the right path of God's plan for us. We both were excited and ready to move on for whatever God's next plan was for us. There was a night after we both agreed upon the decision. We both knelt down before our bed and prayed together like this:

> Dear Father, we are open and ready to accept whatever You prepare for us. Father, we want to thank You for the amazing work from *no* to *yes* and surrendering to Your will totally. It doesn't matter if the baby is Asian, Black, or Caucasian. Whatever You provide for us, we will be happy to accept.

We prayed until tears flowed down on our faces. It's the mixed feelings of joy and thankful hearts. After we accepted the idea, we were able to talk about this new idea and didn't mind to talk to friends about it. We were very excited and awaited God's plan for us.

Previously, we didn't want to talk about the adoption because emotionally and spiritually, we were just not ready to face it. But now, we were free to talk about it. A few friends had asked us if we are going to adopt an Asian, Black, or Caucasian baby. Again, we gave the same answers: "Whatever God prepares for us, we will be happy to accept. We have no preferences." At that point, we really didn't mind at all. I felt the joy, freedom, and relief from bias or prejudices. That includes the narrow-minded cultural background.

The beauty of the new perspective of adoption in godly view from Pastor McGrew's suggestion or idea was very helpful. I'd say that casual visit made a huge impact on our lives. What a rich blessing from God through dear Pastor McGrew's visit. I think that was God's intention and grand plan for us. I suppose that before he passed away, he would have never known what blessing seeds he had planted in our lives. I wished I could have had a chance to thank him in person for his special ministry that had impacted our lives. Thank you, Pastor McGrew. Besides God, you don't know how your ministry has deeply touched my heart and my life, especially in my Christian walk even to this day!

By now, from our past interaction with Pastor McGrew, I was convinced and can tell that in many respects of our interactions that he is really a good minister of God and a faithful servant to Him. I believe that he prays for everything in his ministry and prayed before his coming to our house as well. Many people's lives changed because of the influence of his visit. In Pastor Chuck Smith's Bible teaching, he said the same idea, that in our life and daily activities, the Holy Spirit convicts us to be sensitive and respond to His convictions or nudging. Pastor Charles Stanley has said the same thing: simply obey regardless of your understanding. Pastor McGrew has shared for us about the lesson of the truth of *totally surrendering before God*. It has built the ultimate strong, solid foundation for my future path ahead. Very interesting, Pastor McGrew has also used the mathematical illustration principle to help me with the "prerequisite matter." He said that without learning the basic skill of 2+2=4 in school, we can't move on, such as multiplication or division and so forth. Interestingly, later on, the illustration of the "prerequisite matter" became my helpful guidance to organize my plans and activities in general. The same is the true for all Christians. He emphasized that the first and foremost lesson to learn is "surrender completely before God!"

"Dear Father, we are ready to accept Your plan. Now, we don't know how to start and where to go." I had been praying for specific questions of how and when? "Father God, You knew our hearts are totally willing to accept whatever You provide for us. Lord, please show us what to do and where to turn specifically."

I prayed persistently, specifically for the how and when, daily for exactly two weeks in a row. Interestingly enough, exactly two weeks later, out of the blue, I was surprised to receive a letter from Taiwan. The letter was written by my dear aunt (who would be almost 102 years young in September 2021). In her letter, she said that she talked to my older sister Ka-ju and her husband, I-Tien Chiu. On her visit, she talked to them about the idea of what about bearing another child for us to raise. It was originally her idea, and then she talked to my sister and her husband. I didn't know their conversation exactly, which was the purpose for her visit and the main topic she covered in her letter. According to her letter, she said that both of them agreed upon her idea. At the time, they had four beautiful children, and that's all they wanted—no more children.

Back then my dear sister was around forty years old. They both basically said okay and wanted to give it a try. The main concerned was that their youngest boy was seven years old. She was concerned as to whether she would even be able to get pregnant. That was the big concern to them.

In regard to my aunt's letter, it was totally shocking and surprising. My first question was, is that the way from God in response to my two weeks of praying of *how*, or was that only a coincidence? This was an interesting and challenging question to us. I started to pray and ask God for confirmation.

In the meantime, I wrote them a letter. I made it clear that she should simply take it easy. If she could get pregnant, that's fine. If she's unable to do it, that was also perfectly fine. The key point was that during the waiting time, we didn't do anything but patiently wait and pray. The biggest concern to me was that my sister's health had to be good. That was my main concern. On the other hand, I knew for sure that our ultimate confidence was based in our ultimate provider and our ultimate Maker.

At first, I wrote the letter to thank my dear sister and her husband for their thoughtfulness and kindness. This was beyond just loving-kindness. Their motivation was simply out of great concern for me and was out of their self-sacrificial love for me, for us. We had confidence that this was God's plan for giving us a child. Despite any difficulties, I really had total confidence that she would get pregnant.

After my last letter to my brother-in-law, I emphasized and repeated those important issues to them. It seemed that besides prayer, simply wait patiently and faithfully for God's guidance. While we were in a waiting period for the unknown situation in the future, I had the particular two questions, *when* and *how*, in my prayers. Amazingly enough, all I had been doing was turning to scriptures, and I continued to pray without ceasing. Nothing had happened after my last letter to my sister, but about six or seven months later, something very special happened.

It was on a Tuesday that we received more mail. While I was sorting through the mails, amazingly, I found a total surprise letter from Taiwan. I opened it and noticed that on the top left corner, I saw the very first word that was written in English. It spelled, "CONGRATULATIONS!" All were in capital letters. Then the letter said that my sister was pregnant.

Without a thought, I just looked at those capital letters. I knew what was going on. I didn't even know why, at the moment I glanced at those capital letters, I immediately heard myself screaming and went crazy. I admit that I was really kind of out of control. I think I want to describe the episode about that kind of crazy act behind that surprising, shocking news. It was 100 percent totally unexpected. I received that letter after quite a while, at least seven months after the time. It had happened around the time we both really, completely, joyfully, and freely accepted God's provision, regardless of what race the baby was—Black, White, Asian, etc. Mentally and emotionally speaking, our minds and thoughts were still waiting with a peace. The baby matter was kind of out of a in our life.

At that time, I was talking with one of my best friends, Carolyn, on the phone. While I was opening the mail, she heard me screaming. She said, "Yolanda, did you cut your finger?" (because it had happened before).

"No," I said. "Carolyn, we are going to have a baby next year."

She said, "Are you pregnant?"

"No," I said.

She replied, "I don't get it."

I replied to her, "You don't have to. Just don't worry about it" (I knew that it's hard to explain to her at the time).

Right after I hung up on her, I started to call all of my friends one by one. In the meantime, I felt strongly that I also felt that I had a strong crazy idea that I was even thinking about wanting to take a microphone and announce to the whole world that we are going to have a baby next year. Emotionally, I admitted that I really went crazy. It was hard to control my excitement about the sudden remarkable news. In a sense, I strongly felt as if the doctor had told me, "Yolanda, you are pregnant!" My feeling was totally and genuinely overwhelmed with the surprise about the exciting news.

Guess what! The last one I called was my husband because I knew him well and how he was going to react about this news. I didn't want him to discourage me and kill my joyful, excited mood. But I knew I had to call him. Therefore, out of those names on my calling list, I finally called him at work and told him the same good news. As I predicted, though I couldn't see him, but from the way he responded, he was simply surprised and said, "Oh." It sounded weird and strange.

I didn't say anything. I asked him, "Aren't you happy?"

Then he replied, "Yes, oh, yes, I am happy."

I told myself. "Good thing that I didn't call him first. Otherwise, I am afraid that his reaction would cut down my excited and joyful spirit."

The day he came home, he was acting unusually strange and quiet. I knew that his inside was struggling and wrestling about this sudden surprising news. Again, I was a little disappointed but very understanding about how he felt in his mixed feelings. I thought, *I have experienced that kind of inner conflict as well. I should be more supportive.* I was pretty quiet and didn't want to talk to him about this particular issue in case it caused him to be upset.

I remember there is an article titled "Who Is the Best Teacher?" I thought it was an interesting question, so it must have an interesting answer. But the answer seems quite simple and short: "Your own experience!"

I have found out that it is very true and an interesting answer. A friend of mine said, "Experience is very expensive sometimes." It's very true again to me. Sometimes there are high consequences to pay, and other times, the cost of the consequences may be too high to pay or there could be nothing you can do to pay but only feel regrets for the rest of your life. What a sad tragedy! In fact, the results were nothing they could do to save or change but live with the pain for the rest of their lives. What a good illustration! It's always a good principle to think of the consequence before we act and speak.

So far, God has guided each one of us in His ways and His unique timing. And remarkably, He proceeded and guided us step-by-step. That was based on His timing and different paces for the two of us together. In the same time, God also made us to learn separately and individually as well. In reality, from what I have learned through this complicated encounter during the detail-processing. I understood and believed what the Bible says in my head, but it's so much different to learn and understand through my own experiences. Because in so doing, it's in that actual walking through every turning and step-by-step that we are able to get a chance to sense, to observe, and to learn firsthand. The *Word* of God becomes more alive in a deeper meaning in my mind. For example, I remember after I had chanced a visit to Jerusalem, Israel, and seen many historical places in biblical times. The most memorable were these two places: the empty tomb in the cave (the actual spot where Jesus's dead body laid [in fact, I don't know why, but when I walked inside the cave, I was in tears—maybe because Jesus's extreme physical torture just struck my mind]) and Jesus's birthplace, the manger surrounded by sheep. I have much deeper sense, feeling, and array of thoughts in my mind ever since. I know that the Word of God is alive and more real, in a sense. In general, by faith, I do totally believe God's Word even though I don't understand many parts of it. My point is that our personal experience does make the result different in general.

We knew now that God's way for giving us the baby was from my sister. In other words, it was a confirmation from God, who answered our prayers. We had to wait for about nine months for the baby to be born. Emotionally, during this long waiting period, what we needed was more faith than effort. That is why I was very careful to pay attention to my behavior toward Jacob, my husband, just to make sure I didn't say things to upset Him. I told him that he can take it easy and no need to be anxious because it's going to take a little while before the baby is born.

I remember that it was on a Tuesday, the day after Columbus Day, that I received the letter about my sister's pregnancy. But on that Thursday evening, only two days later, when I came home from school, when I first walked to the house, he was acting exceptionally and unusually gentle. He carefully took a few books and looked at me strangely. He said to me with a very calm and serious attitude, "Whoomy"—that's what my folks call me—"I want to tell you that until now, today, I truly realized and actually felt very happy about the baby's coming."

The tears ran down on his face. His unusual and strange behavior was absolutely shocking to me. I was in awe, with goose bumps instantly, and I didn't know what to say! How could that be again? This was only two days after the good news. In my mind, I thought that a stubborn, hardheaded man like him most likely would take him at least two or three months or at least a few weeks. I totally couldn't believe what I had seen and heard. That's why I got goose bumps simultaneously. It was 100 percent out of my expectation and understanding.

At the same time, I truly felt the Holy Spirit's actual presence. It was so real to the point that I could have even touched the Spirit with my hands. Even now, at this very moment while I am writing this, it's still fresh as I remember back then. At first, the Spirit was working in me alone and then separately in my husband. Although I have had several encounters and experiences with the Spirit's amazing acts, again, it was just another miracle (another exceptional blessing because of the sake of learning the lesson of completely surrendering before God). Ironically, in so doing, I have seen firsthand the concrete evidence of what He promised. In reality, the battle belongs to Him, and so does the victory.

Regarding his very unusual reactions toward me in only two days, I really think that was absolutely very strange behavior for his usually stubborn personality and was out of my understanding. There are no words that I could use to describe the situation. The only way to explain is that it was totally under the Holy Spirit's will and conviction. (I remember vividly an incident that had happened to me quite a while back. It was exactly the same situation. I noticed that how I was acting and what I was saying were not on my carnal way, but the spiritual-filled way.) For a few minutes, I was still in awe and told myself that this is unbelievable. This can't be true. It's simply amazing.

This is another incident of the Spirit's mighty work at first, God worked with me only, then working at him later. In other words, God worked separately with us individually, at different times. I was reacting crazy excited first, and two days later, he came around. Again, it's another miracle, another exceptional blessing because of the sake of learning to utterly surrender to His will.

When I was thinking it through carefully, summing up from all of the details of the experience or encountering, I realized that even though each story was different, I'd say that it's about the same pattern, the same type. Most likely, it began with the unwillingness to struggle for yearning to cling to the truth and to develop a closer relationship with God. As always, all of the experiences that happened most likely began with the self-will choice in the beginning of the issue, the decision to relinquish the original firm decision. And finally, in the end, in so doing, God won the battle through our total submission to His will design plan after the lesson we learned "Completely surrender before Him." Ironically, in so doing, I have seen the concrete evidence firsthand of what He has promised. In reality, the battle belongs to Him, and so does the victory. Dr. Charles Stanley once said that God will send the right amount of pressure to position you for surrender and blessing. That very much depicts the encounter of the whole story.

Regarding the *barren* issue, due to the long-term suffering from my deep depression issue and feeling a strong sense of emptiness deep inside of me, those mixed feelings have totally overwhelmed me for a while. Emotionally speaking, I had no other resources to ask for help and neither able to receive any spiritual support. The key was unable to share my inner pains and the saddest part was that I was all alone with no one that I could share my misery. Therefore, the only one I could complain to, blame, and express my anger, my disappointment, and discouragement to was our loving God. Back then, the so-called "all-loving, all-knowing, and all-powerful God" wasn't what He was for me in that time frame. To me, this was the God in my heart who I thought He had been. I still vividly remember to this day what I said to Him, every word of it. I have complained and blamed Him and been very angry toward Him for all my inner emotional misery. These are the cruel, hostile words and attitude I had toward Him:

> What kind of God are You? You discriminated against me. How long are You going to ignore me? You are so called the Almighty God. There are lots of people when they get married, they don't even have to pray, and You automatically give them children for free. But why not me? Oh, God, You know me well, that I am that particular person who loves the children so very much. You know that I have been praying and praying to the point of practically going insane, staying in the depths of sadness and self-pity and deep depression for so long! Yet You ignored my praying, crying, heart-wrenching, and begging. But You still kept silent to me! Oh, God, since You don't care for me, I think that I am going to believe another god.

To this day I still vividly remember every single word I had said back then. I remember well that when I was at my extremely lowest point emotionally and spiritually, I really lost my patience, and I even had lost my sanity. My life was simply miserable and had a great sense of emptiness and discouragement! So desperately longing for a child, it was practically haunting me constantly, days and nights, nonstop, just about 24-7 for years.

When I thought about what I had said, those unkind and bitter words to our Lord, I just couldn't stop the tears flowing down. I couldn't stop feeling guilty and ashamed. Regardless, He knew and understood that I was in a terrible mental state in my life. I also knew for a fact that He totally forgave my misconduct and loved me for who I was. But that part of me still felt bad and ashamed. In the end, He completely wiped off my tears and is still telling me that He loves me and accepts me and forgives me unconditionally.

And that's why the same night of that special day, it was the Holy Spirit empowering and convicting me so deeply and touching my soul and my heart. I was sobbing and feeling so guilty, so ashamed of myself, and I just couldn't forgive myself. I asked for His mercy and forgiveness in comparison to what I had done, for my shameful and ugly attitude toward Him. I didn't expect Him to forgive me because I felt undeserving and unworthy to accept His Love and His forgiveness. Through it all, the miraculous, amazing incidents just happened over and over again. Those were not happening by coincidence. Like Pastor Jon Courson said, "Nothing is accidental to us as Christians."

Through it all, When I think hard about those very details and painful experiences, I finally figured out the reason for the uncontrollable, inexplicable sobbing, crying out loud. Through it all, I know that I was convicted by the Holy Spirit through His powerful, unshakable Word.

> For God did not send his Son to condemned the
> world, but to save. (John 3:17)

> As far as the east is from the west, so far has he removed my transgressions from me. (Psalm 103:12)

Indeed, God is always faithful, as He says He is. I believed and accepted His perfect, graceful cleanse and shower upon me. Thank You, Lord, for being who You say you are.

Because of all the wrong behaviors that I had done to Him for so long, I felt I couldn't forgive myself. But I knew for a fact that it is simply by His *grace*. The Bible says that grace is unmerited and undeserved. We can simply freely receive and accept His perfect Love. And that's exactly why it triggered me to cry so hard. Jesus loves me and accepts me unconditionally while I was a sinner. Even on this particular incident, I have been mad and harboring grudges and complaining, whining in my heart for a long time. But regardless, He still loved me in spite of my disobedience and my childish behavior, which led me to betray Him. He totally forgave my sins and unconditionally loved and accepted me. Even though I was once like a prodigal daughter, once having turned my back and even rejected Him with my bitter words. Thanks to God for Jesus. Because of Him, I know for a fact that I am able to receive the free gift of *grace*. That means "as far as the east is from the west, so far has he removed my transgressions from me" (Psalm 103:12).

One of the most important things in my life was to have six children. My parents had a "dirty dozen"—twelve children. I have told God that I only want six children. In reality, I had none. And that was the main issue: from expecting to have six children to having none, not even one child. It was a main issue that having a child was the most important thing after I got married.

The biblical viewpoint is if we love anything more than we love God, that's wrong. That meant that I had been acting very wrong as a Christian all the time, yet I didn't realize it, and I kept on doing the wrong thing without knowing what the truth was. I loved to have a child more than I love and obeyed God. To have a child was just everything in my life after I got married. That's why I was so miserable In other words, God knew that the priority in my Christian life was wrong. In effect, after I truly acknowledged, corrected, and changed my priority, I finally figured out what it "Him first—salvation begins with death to myself" meant. This is a basic, fundamental truth at all times.

He used His unique way to discipline me and guide me to learn how to surrender completely before Him. With a very thankful and joyful heart, I give my thanks to the Lord that it was through the work of the Holy Spirit; He has helped me in His way to learn to obey Him with the sincere heart of a cheerful and self-sacrificial attitude. For fact, it's absolutely no regret in my heart and mind. In my practical life, I felt that God had given me a new heart, new thinking, and new life—brand-new priority ever since. I became a new person when I accepted Christ. The old one is dead. "Therefore, if anyone is in Christ, he is a new creation; the old one has gone, the new has come" (2 Corinthians 5:17).

*A brief conclusion*

These three amazing incidents that had happened on the same day made a tremendous impact for the rest of my life. The longtime hidden secret had been willfully continuing to remain in the secret spot, but it was suddenly broken and opened up utterly and surprisingly. The feelings of the perpetually strong idea or the rigid concept of longing for a child had miraculously vanished or disappeared at the time. Finally, first and foremost, the key point in my life was to learn complete surrender before Him. It was firmly acknowledged and deeply committed in my prayers, crying out loud verbally, along with tears flowing down my cheeks. I was fully determined to apply this practice for the rest of my life.

I believe that Christianity is the partnership between divine sovereignty and human responsibility, going hand in hand. I believe and know that this is the moment depicting my situation now. In other words, I did my part, did my responsibility to comply with His conviction. I felt totally relieved and refreshed spiritually and emotionally. I believe Christianity is a partnership because some areas are

God's business that only He can do. We can't do or help God's jobs that belong to Him alone, that only He can.

Likewise, there are some areas that are our responsible to take care of. God won't do it for us or help us. What a profound insight to remember and to practice. What an awesome, wonderful day. It was a victorious and richly blessed day from the Lord in His plan and His way. Thank You, Lord. You alone deserve all the praise and glory. He accomplished it all by Himself according to His will and His pleasure (Psalm 46:9–10).

Finally, the long and complicated journey of the adoption: we know the *where* and the *when* questions after having prayed for two weeks in a row. It was God's timing and guidance. Surely, the baby is to come from my sister and her husband.

Thank You, Lord, for answering our prayers in the way You have planned for us.

> I determined the exact time of your birth and where you would live. (Acts 17:26)
>
> I chose you when I planned creation. (Ephesians 1:11).

I still remember vividly that the lady from my early church said that children are all gifts from God regardless where they come from. It's so true indeed! Although Naomi our daughter and George our son are from different people and different times, regardless, they still were under God's perfect timing and special, unique ways.

While I was writing the adoption issue, one day, I was studying the Bible in Genesis 1:1–20 regarding God's creation. After God had completed His six-day creation, He saw all that He made and said it was good. When I read that, I thought God is not only our God, the sovereign and Almighty God, but He has a sense of humor too! I thought that was very interesting! He admired His own masterpiece after the sixth day of creation. God saw all that He had made, and it was very good (Genesis 1:31).

I didn't know why at that moment, I just thought God was an invisible human being like us too. I felt that He is a real being and very approachable. Although I have never seen Him, I also felt He was an emotional and spiritual *being* just like me. At the same time, God is also an orderly God. He does things according to His plans and His priority. He waited to finish His own creations, and then in His final step and perfect timing, He created Adam and Eve. "God said, let us make man in our image, in our likeness and let them rule" (Genesis 1:26). God knew those creations were needed and required by the human beings.

It caused me to think about the illustration of the newborn baby coming and how the new mother prepares for this important event, especially for the first pregnancy. She spends a lot of time preparing for everything that the baby will need. Likewise, I understand God's perfect six-day creation very much illustrates the story of the good preparation for the adoption of our daughter Naomi and later on, our son George.

God had well prepared me before I even knew what was going on. He had it all figured out from the very beginning to the end. I still vividly remember that after Pastor McGrew gave a significant lesson. The same idea spoke to me. Before Pastor McGrew' visit, I never heard of or received the surrendering-to-God issue as a theoretical teaching. The focal point is that without learning the precious lesson of completely surrendering before Him as my basic and foremost biblical teaching, there wouldn't have been those miracle stories after the stories. All those small or complicated stories were strictly based on that particular profound principal of completely surrendering before Him. It simply couldn't move on. The same idea is present in math—that if we don't learn the basic principles of addition and subtraction, how can we move on to deeper-level knowledge or skills? This is just the sequence or prerequisite formula. In college, you know that if you don't take certain classes as a basic or prerequisite class, you won't be able to advance to the next one.

I want to give a huge thanks to Pastor McGrew, who was sent by God to help us to learn this basic, significant lesson: *surrender completely before God!*

The key element is that with this vital brand-new lesson, as a very basic biblical component in my Christian walk. It was an extremely helpful principle to strengthen my Christian journey in the years to come. I didn't know why, but it made me think about one of my favorite songs, "Is Your All on the Altar?" The following is a quote from the chorus:

> Is your all on the altar of sacrifice laid? Your heart
> does the Spirit control? You can only be blest and
> have peace and sweet rest as you yield Him your
> body and soul.

Both melody and words are absolutely beautiful with deep meaning. Sometimes, I love to sing it to myself and to God with my heart. I found that it is very enjoyable and connects my emotions to my soul as well. Oftentimes, I sing it with tears flowing, which gives healing and sooths my inner being emotionally and spiritually. I felt that I was closer to God and was able to connect to His Spirit in a deeper sense.

Now, I'd like to quote these two scriptures as the final conclusion for the two particular adoptions of my son, George, and my daughter, Naomi, because they depict and match this episode remarkably and amazingly.

> I chose you when I planned my creation.
> (Ephesians 1:11)

> I determined the exact time of your birth and
> where you would live. (Acts 17:26)

Thank You, Lord, for answering our prayers, which was the way You directed us to Your specific grand plan for us. The questions of where and how were clearly and firmly answered regarding the adoption issue. Thank You for Your wonderful, remarkable works, which only YOU alone are able to fulfill for YOUR ultimate grand plan for us.

# Completely Surrender before God, Part 3 Obeying without Understanding The Actual Stories for the Baby's Coming to US

*How the baby's coming from a president's special bill!*

I'd like to quote one of my favorite sayings, "God won't give you an assignment without giving you the proper tools you need." The story has been exactly confirmed with this scripture: "God's strength always matches your days" (Deuteronomy 33:25 I paraphrased). I am the living proof! Because I personally have experienced this numerous times in my Christian walk. To this day, I try to remember it in my heart and put into practice my lifetime reminder in my daily life.

Back to the story. The day after Columbus Day, we heard the good news about my sister's being pregnant, so the baby will be born sometime in May or June of the next year. Interestingly, before we had known or planned anything about the baby's matter, my husband, Jacob, was working at General Electric company as an industrial engineer. His company's annual shutdown has always been in June. That means that all the employees were required to take their vacation in June only, so we made our plans to go back to Taiwan to visit. This was our first time since we came to the United States. Amazing, isn't it? Naomi was born on May 30, 1976.

It was also our great country America's two hundredth anniversary. At the time, I was still working on my graduate school, but I stopped schooling. I went back to Taiwan before the baby was born. Jacob went back in June during the company's shutdown period.

Jacob named her Naomi as an English name and named her *Jehreh* as the Mandarin name. *Jehreh* is a biblical name from Exodus 14:14. It means "God provides, and God prepares" (I took the Mandarin Bible version translation). I teased him that giving the name of *Jehreh* was the best pick, or perfect choice in his whole life, since I have known him because that's the perfect meaning and exactly fits her coming into the world. It was just beautiful and also a perfect fit in God's plan. I give all the thanks and praises for His divine provisions and preparations. It's also so true to confirm what the scripture says, "I say, 'My purpose will stand, and I will do all that I please'" (Isaiah 46:10b) and "what I have said, that will I bring about; what I have planned, that will I do" (Isaiah 46:11b). Indeed, Father God, *You* started, and You finished well and completed. Thanks to God, that *You* are really faithful and mighty as You said *who You are*, the *all-knowing, the all-powerful,* and *the all-loving God* of the whole universe.

I spent about two months in Taiwan with her, and Jacob stayed in Taiwan about one month. We both were just thrilled and felt great joy with the tiny baby girl, our new daughter Naomi. Jacob loved and enjoyed to be with our new baby dearly and enjoyed to be her new dad.

As for me, in my whole life, it was the greatest time that I truly enjoy my life as a new mother. I felt I was a different person in many areas that I didn't know before I became a mother. I'd say that this was the most fulfilling and joyful and meaningful time in my life. Now, in reality, I started to apply for her visa so that I can bring her with me to the US. To my total surprise, I couldn't bring her with me at the time. That unexpected bad news was absolutely sad and disappointing and surprising. We were heartbroken, feeling terribly sad and confused. After I stayed with her for two months, it was very hard for me to be separated and leave her in Taiwan and come home empty-handed. In the plane, I cried and felt terribly sad all the way with puzzling and perplexing thoughts.

Logically and naturally, I asked God, "Why and what's the reason that the story turned out this way?" Jacob's reaction to the disappointment was much harder on him than me. He kept asking me why. It doesn't make sense that God had made us wait for so long, and finally, He gave us a precious baby girl, and we couldn't bring her with us.

We couldn't enjoy that babyhood's fun time or adorable, precious stages. As a matter of fact, I didn't know why that although I felt disappointed and kind of sad, however, the inside of my attitude toward the reality, I felt that it seemed God had a purpose or allowed it to happen this way for a purpose. I didn't know why, yet I took it much calmly and peacefully emotionally. I encouraged myself and continued to be obedient to Him and trust that He knows what He was doing. It seemed that I strongly felt that with the first precious lesson we had just learned, completely surrender before God, as my solid foundational base, it really helped me a great deal. However, we were both feeling disappointed and sad, though not falling apart or crushed spiritually and emotionally. I'd like to credit the great lesson that we have both had just learned: surrender before God. As a result, we still accept it and try to accept the attitude of "Obeying without understanding," as our Christian walk. We took the bold step to carry on our normal activities in our life. Thanks to God for sending Pastor McGrew's great messages and lesson, his fundamental truth encouraging and reminding us. It made this ordeal much easier.

Sometimes, there were some Christian friends who like to ask us why is that God's will, and how come that turned out this way? It doesn't make sense in our logical human viewpoint. It didn't matter. The most important is that we were confident that God was in charge and was totally in His good hand. I have found the best answer is from His own words:

> No one can comprehend what goes on under the
> sun. Despite his efforts to search it out, no one

can discover its meaning. Even if the wise man claim they know, he cannot really comprehend it. (Ecclesiastes 8:17)

I think that no one can give better answer than that.

I also thought about an interesting answer that I had mentioned in the other article. One day, I saw on TV that someone was talking to the well-known evangelist and preacher Dr. Billy Graham. He was asked this question: "You are a great evangelist, not only in America but also in the world. Do you have questions that you don't have the answer to?"

Without any hesitation, he answered, "Oh, yes, I have made a long list I will ask my Lord one day when I go to see Him in person." The same was true for us in our situation. We not only felt perplexed, but we didn't know what to do, yet we kept on obeying and trusting that God's up to something. We simply didn't know what. However, we continued to live our life based on the belief of "obeying without understanding." In the meantime, we kept on praying for God's help and guidance for what to do.

I just remember this interesting saying: "When life is easy, we don't have a problem, but when life is tough, we don't have an answer." As for me, as a Christian, I think we have the perfect answer from Jesus. He said, "In this world you are going to have problems, setbacks, tribulations, but since I have overcome the world, if you come to me, you can too" (John 16:32 I paraphrased). As we have said all the time, nothing is too big or too hard for Jesus!

Sometimes, facing the reality can be very tough and challenging. I think this is one of those tough times. Regardless, I quit my job and school and went back to visit her in Taiwan about every two or three months, staying about one or two months. According to the US immigration law, the two years staying with her can be separate visits in several times as long as it fulfills the two-year in totality. I had a wonderful time with her on each visit. We just enjoyed being together as mother and daughter. I felt we were bonding and developing a good relationship. She was very smart, happy, and mature for her age and was friendly and enjoyed being around other people.

After we came back from Taiwan on the first visit, one day, we just decided to go to see Pastor McGrew for help and for prayers. Pastor McGrew was a very good listener. He listened attentively, even the very details of the whole story from very beginning to the end. At last, we were asking help for the big issue regarding being unable to get the baby's visa to come to our country.

In Taiwan, I had worked hard to legally adopt her as our legally adopted daughter. Ever since, legally, she became our adoptive daughter in Taiwan. But the American embassy in Taipei, Taiwan, rejected it for the reason that she wasn't considered an orphan because her parents were alive and healthy. Back then, according to immigration law, in our case, one of us or both are required to stay with her for two years in Taiwan. Without fulfilling that legal requirement, the case was closed. In reality, that's simply hard for us to comply with, and that's the reason we went to see Pastor McGrew for prayers and for help.

After we told him every detail of the whole story and the processing from the beginning until the baby was born, Pastor McGrew was very touched by our amazing and unusual story. He said to me, "Yolanda, this coming Sunday, I am not going to preach. I want you to share your beautiful story to our congregation."

To be honest, my first reaction was, "Are you crazy?" Of course, I could not tell him how I felt. Instead, I responded to him politely, "Oh, no, I can't do that."

He said to me, "Why not?"

I gave a few good excuses to turn him down and even told him that I couldn't speak English. He said to me, "You just did. Since I understood, our congregation will understand as well."

Regardless, Pastor McGrew did not give up. He was persistent. Somehow, I could tell that he was smart enough to perceive my inner struggles to share my story. He finally said to me, "Yolanda, you have to understand that you are not doing this for you but for Him alone."

That's the key point. Suddenly, I felt that despite any obstacles and excuses, I had to do it. I just wanted to surrender to do it for God's sake, not for me.

Even though I still didn't want to, I finally was obedient and told him, "Okay."

The day before the service started, he led us to pray. Something strange had happened. All the inner fear—afraid of failing, being embarrassed, that I won't do a good job, etc.—all those awful frightening feelings suddenly disappeared. Simply gone! I felt totally at peace and not even nervous at all.

I walked few steps to the pulpit, and the moment I began to speak, I noticed that the sanctuary was full of more than about one hundred congregants, but still I was calm. I asked myself how come I was not nervous or afraid at all.

On the pulpit, I faced our congregation, spoke to foreigners, and even spoke in English. It simply did not matter; it didn't bother me at all. I started to talk with ease and absolute calm, which was amazing. The sinful-nature part of me wondered, questioning, *How can this be? This is impossible, but in reality, it's happening now.* It's totally amazing how beautifully and smoothly I spoke. I honestly had a hard time believing that it was me speaking. This was the very first time in my entire life that I had made it through so naturally without even realizing that I was speaking to more than one hundred people and was in English. This was a foreign language to me! Absolutely amazing! I was virtually forgetting about the fear of failure, and not even felt nervous—period! This was another evidence to prove that when the Spirit is having His way, we act and do according to His ways without even realizing it. Indeed, it's another evidence to prove the wonderful miraculous work of the Holy Spirit!

Now, I want to explain why I continually refused Pastor McGrew's invitation. First, I am a shy, introverted person. From my previous all times of failing experiences as a student in school, I totally lost my confidence. It may be called stage fright.

It came to pass that our congregation now understood much better about the situation of the adoption issue. At this point, besides prayers, Pastor McGrew also encouraged our congregation to write to our local congressmen for this special situation. In fact, there were more than ten people who, out of their kindness, had written the letters on our behalf. Unfortunately, all of them received the same answers from the American embassy in Taiwan. Another disappointment, but at least we tried. We appreciated their actual action of helping.

The new reality was the moving issue. Moving from Chicago, Illinois, to California was an enormous change in many aspects. In reality, my first concern was to find a house in the place where I had never heard: the city of Riverside, California. During that time, I was still in school, working on my graduate program. At the same time, I also wanted to take a class after the one-week break, so I had to find a house to buy in only one week. It was a tough time and tough issue, but I had no choice.

As always, I remembered the word *pray!* I knew for a fact that moving to Riverside was God's plan for us. He will help us find a house even in a week. Of course, God knew all my limits and all the details concerning this situation. Jacob's company *Bourns* was pretty nice. They actually bought me a ticket to come to Riverside to look for a house. The company had arranged for us to stay at the Hilton Hotel and sent a good realtor to pick me up to search for a house on the following day.

*Searching day 1*

Jacob and I had told the realtor about a few main ideas of what we were looking for. One of the items was we preferred to have a two-story house. The house we had in Chicago was one story. It would be nice to have a two-story house. On the first day, the realtor had prepared six houses to check out that fit our desires. At the time, I did not know what areas were good or bad. Later on, I knew that those five houses were in the best areas, called Canyon Crest. It was also considered a prestigious area. The last one was on Blaine. It was considered the second-best area.

After we looked through all of them, he asked me, "What do I think, and which one do you like the most?"

As we were driving back to the hotel, he turned to Spruce Street from Blaine, which was the last house we looked at. He said, "Well, that's all I have for today. Maybe tomorrow we will have more to look at. Did you like any of them?"

I said no. He asked why. I said to him, "I don't know, but when I see what I want, I could tell right away." I then snapped my fingers before him. That means I can tell right away.

Believe it or not, only within a couple of minutes, I suddenly noticed that on our left side, there was a for-sale sign in the front yard. He said, "That is not in my book. It must be very new." We stopped, and he went to check with the owner.

While he was out of the car, I took a good look at the house. Just those few minutes, believe it or not, I fell in love with that house. I even felt strongly that this was the house God had provided and prepared for us. It's called love at first sight. It was a two-story house, which was our ideal one. I didn't know why. I simply loved the outside look of the house.

The realtor came back laughing and said, "Let's go."

While we were walking toward the house, I asked myself the question, just kind of curious wanted know what's the inside of the house will like. The moment as I walking into the house, I just loved it. The carpet was green and still very nice even to this day. It was both our number one favorite color. Immediately, the question was, "How much?" His answer was around $78,800. Guess what? Our budget was $80,000! *Bingo!* Praise the Lord! I found the ideal dream house on the first day of searching. All I have been worrying and panicking over concerns were really unnecessary at all.

It was an unbelievable miracle! In the beginning, I was worried that it would be impossible. But now, my dream came true nice and easy at the very first day. How about that? It was absolutely amazing! Looking back at the beginning, we simply prayed! The real evidence was confirmed and proved over and over again that God orchestrated every single step of the way. What a mighty miraculous work, Father God! *You* alone deserve all the praises and glory.

During the purchasing period, there was another interesting episode behind the story. Although it might be considered a petty thing, it also played a key element as well. During my one week looking for the house, there were two other interested parties who were hired by the same company. They needed to buy a house as well. We heard that both parties would like to buy the same house very much as well. They had actually looked at the house before we did, but they were waiting for their spouses to come before making an official offer. While those parties were waiting, we made the official offer and got the house before their decisions. The realtor said that we were just the lucky buyers. To me, it was God's perfect timing, perfect reservation for us. It was God working on our behalf and working every detail out at every step of the way.

Now the next step was moving. Jacob moved into our new house in the summertime because he began to work in June. I moved to Riverside six months later before Thanksgiving Day. I also completed all my academic courses, even able to turn in my thesis. It was all because of the moving. At least I did not have to go to school anymore. I stayed in Chicago until l sold our house.

In regard to the complication of the adoption, one day after I came back from Taiwan, I visited a dear neighbor, Evelyn, who lived across the street from our house. She was a pretty lady, friendly, nice, and kind. Jacob told me that when the moving truck from Chicago arrived at our house in the morning, she brought breakfast stuff over to our home. We were very thankful and blessed for having such a considerate neighbor. The day after I came back from Taiwan, I went to visit her just to say hello as a friendly courtesy visit.

While I was visiting, she anxiously asked me, "Where is your daughter? Why didn't you bring her with you?"

I then told her the complicated problems of the whole story. She told me that I should try it again since we are now in California, a different state from Illinois. I said to her that I have. I also said to her, "Evelyn, there was no need to try it again. They would have told us the same information." As a matter of fact, I did write to Sen. Alan Cranston and our local congressman George Brown. The attorney in Mr. Brown's office replied to me the same information as I have heard in Taiwan and Chicago, but I have never received a response from Senator Cranston.

The following information was the key factor that would open the door for the whole issue. It was the first step. Somehow, I felt there was a thought that came from the Holy Spirit's revelation. I continued, unless I can meet the important people in person, it would be a waste of time. Thank God! He was giving me the wisdom and discernment to mention to her. Amazingly, Evelyn responded immediately and called her next-door neighbor Sara to come over right away. She told her on the phone, "Yolanda wants to tell you about an important issue she is facing."

As we were discussing the problems of the situation, guess what happened. Interestingly enough, I especially said that we personally need to have a special connection to meet a VIP, otherwise, it's not going to work. In essence, it perfectly turned out that way. With God's special blessing, we actually found a perfect VIP. Thank You, Lord, for Your mysterious provision! Guess what. Sara does have a friend who works for our local congressman George Brown as a secretary. Without Sara's personal connection, we would never have a chance to meet Congressman Brown in person. That was exactly what I had said to Evelyn in the beginning. "Unless we can meet that VIP in person, it'd be waste of time." That was a key factor, and it happened exactly like that! Sara, the next-door neighbor, came over to meet us right away. Evelyn and I told her what's going on with the story.

Previously, I had written a letter to Senator Cranston, but no answers. For a while, one day, out of the blue, early in the morning, while I was still sleeping, there was a phone call. It was a call from the capitol in Sacramento, the secretary of Sen. Alan Cranston. She said that it took a month to receive my letter. Instead of sending me a letter, she'd rather call me. She totally understood that I needed to know the answer as soon as possible. That was very kind and thoughtful of her. This was what she said to me:

> First of all, I am very sorry about your situation. It surely was a beautiful story, but to be honest with you, there was nothing that the senator can do to help out in this matter. But there is one thing I can suggest you to do. Go to your local representative, our district congressman, they are

the ones that can and are able to help you in this
particular matter. Go and ask your congressman
to file a special bill on your behalf.

I asked her, "What does it mean?"

She patiently explained it to me. Praises to the Lord. I was so
grateful to Evelyn, Sara, and her friend Judy for all working together
to help me. Judy made the appointment for us to meet Congressman
Brown. His office was located at downtown Riverside in the historical building Mission Inn.

Mr. Brown was a very kind and humble man. He did not act
like a VIP figure. He was just like a good, ordinary citizen who had
a big heart and was willing to help us in this matter. It was at our
appointment that he told us that he, as our local representative, can
help us to file a special bill to the Judiciary Committee. Yes, sure
enough, that was exactly what Senator Cranston's secretary had told
me on the phone.

When Mr. Brown submitted the special bill to the Judiciary
Committee, the majority of the members would have to decide to
accept it or not. It means that every year, our government allows
each state to have one or two cases that although are in conflict with
the law, if the case is a nice, kind, or humanitarian beautiful case,
they can make an exception and let the Judiciary Committee vote
and decide. So first to congress. If it passes, it goes to the senate,
after that, it goes to the highest step, which is to the president. Back
then, President Carter was the sitting president. This was the general
process and procedure.

Everything seemed to go well. While we met with our congressman Mr. Brown in his office, we told him all the details of our story.
He was very impressed and agreed to do his best to file the special
bill on our behalf.

Thank God, the first and the second step went well and passed.
The final step was also the highest step, which was to President
Carter. He signed the special bill. Congressman Brown brought
the paper with personal signature signed by President Carter, along
with a special pen that said, "The Whitehouse, Jimmy Carter." *Wow!*

What a total surprise and honor. We were overwhelmed and honored to receive such a wonderful, precious gift. It was supernice that Congressman Brown made a special visit to our house and gave us a few precious gifts. We were extremely thankful, honored, and joyful for the results of this whole legal process. The whole process, every detail, was like a fairy-tale story. It was absolutely amazing and remarkable. Almighty God, *You* speak, and it is done. Your words are true. They are powerful, and they really brought the fairy-tale story into a reality in our life.

Suppose we did not buy this particular house on Spruce Street, we would not have met these very special neighbors Evelyn, Sara, and Judy, and also Congressman Brown. If it were not for this very special connection, we would not have been able to bring our daughter Naomi from Taiwan to America. "He who began the good work in you will carry it on the completion" (Philippians 1:6). That reminded me of this scripture that God is always faithful as He says He is.

The *Press-Enterprise*, our local paper, asked our permission to publish our story in the paper. There was a newsman who asked me on the phone. At first, I said *no*. He asked, "Why not?"

I thought that this was a personal story and did not feel comfortable having it published in the paper. The newsman said to me, "There are too many ugly stories of violence, gunshots, horrible stories in the paper all the time. Your story was such a remarkable and beautiful story that people would love to read it." He kind of begged me and tried to persuade me.

I thought that is true, but I still felt awkward. Anyhow, I let them publish it. Surprisingly, there were a few people who saw the story on the papers and brought gifts to our daughter as welcome presents. That was an extranice surprise!

Through it all, I often ponder and think through all the small incidents along the way that have happened since we were both willing to accept God's plan for the adoption. Both adoption cases of our son George and our daughter Naomi's case were the same complicated during the process. The similarity was the same pattern in spite of the different stories. It all began with total obedience to His will from 0 percent *no* to 100 percent *yes* in the end. It was absolutely based on the precious lesson of completely surrendering before God.

During the long, complicated process, there were challenges that happened from time to time. Yet I still persistently stayed in line with His directions and guidance through sincere, fervent prayers. There were times we were confused, perplexed, and struggling even with doubt. "Are we on the right tracks or disconnected from God's plan?" The only way I know for sure was the fact of "the total peace" in my heart. Peace is the sign to indicate and know that I am sure that's God's will and was in His plan. "May the Lord of peace himself give you peace at all times and in every way" (2 Thessalonians 3:16). *Peace* means a holistic sense of well-being built on the foundation of peace with God (Roman 5:1, Philippians 4:7, Colossians 3:15).

In essence, not only the Bible says so, I have actually experienced firsthand myself at all times. Ironically, in all cases, peace is inextricably connected with God's presence. Thank you, Lord, YOU are the Prince of Peace! "Jesus Himself is the Prince of Peace" (Isaiah 9:2–7).

Know Jesus, know peace. No Jesus, no peace! Well-said, great meaning.

# Completely Surrender before God, Part 4

What I said, I will do.

—Isaiah 46:11

Delight yourself in the Lord, and He will
put His desire into your heart.

—Psalm 37:4

He who began a good work, will continue
to carry on till completion.

—Philippians 1:6

In the end, precisely in God's grand plan and in His own very special way, He finally fulfilled my ultimate wish in my very young age. The amazing point was that I had no idea at all. I absolutely didn't have any clue back then. When Pastor McGrew first visited our house in Chicago, he had said many insightful words, including, "Yolanda, when you pray, God gives you what is the *best* for you but not what you *want*. God answers our prayers according to His time and His way but not your time and your way." Great insight!

However, at the time, I simply interpreted it as a pastor's common encouragement to his congregation. It didn't mean much to me.

Life went on fast much later. After I thought of it carefully and pondered through the whole episode, I finally figured out that those messages were God's preplanned messages to me, but I had not known at all, so obviously, Pastor McGrew was the appointed messenger or angel from God to rekindle me and minister to me in my life.

As I mentioned before, I was born to a big family and am the third child from the top. I did have a very strong commitment in my heart that I wanted to fulfill my father's wish when I was a young child. Why and how did that happen? When I was still in the elementary-school age, out of the blue, I remember that my father simply proudly had shown us several certificates that he had earned from his schooltime. He also said that six year in a row, he had made first place in his class all the way.

Back then, Taiwan was reigned by Japanese government for about forty years or so. That means that the official language was Japanese. In simple terms, Japan was the boss, the leader of Taiwan, before World War 2. I was told that the Taiwanese were treated like second-class citizens in general. That was why my father could earn the first place in his class, which was very unusual and proud. My father was a genius before he passed away at the age of seventy-three years old. He could remember 131 phone numbers in his head. True story. Back then, I remember that when I went back to Taiwan, he was my phone book. It worked every time. I love my father and miss him very much. He was always my rock and my hero in my life. To be able to achieve that level was very hard and honored. Subconsciously, I felt that he kind of meant that someday, if we could achieve that level, that will be nice. He also said that someday when we all grow up, those who are better off should help those who have less. Nobody knew besides God. Since then, my strong commitment has been glued and has stayed in my heart regardless!

Later on, with the biblical perspective in view, I really think that I was nudged or convicted by the Holy Spirit's power. The scripture says, "Delight yourself in the Lord, He will put His desire in your heart" (Psalm 37:4). Although my dear father had gone to be with the Lord, those significant, heartfelt words are still as fresh today as back then.

Even I have forgotten myself completely until lately. There were so many things that happened in the last few years. In fact, I believe this statement: "our life is God's story!" From my own real-life journey, I kind of have seen the picture more clearly, slowly, and gradually. Before Pastor McGrew's visit, what I have thought the best thing to me was having a child. However, Pastor McGrew's great insight amazingly opened my spiritual eyes, and it even changed completely God's original grand plan for me in my life, which I didn't even know back then. According to Pastor McGrew's biblical viewpoint, the *best* thing for me to learn was learning to completely surrender before God, not a child. As for me, what I had in mind for my life's goal at my young age was to make more money, lots of money to help my family when I grew up. I like to use the illustration like a puzzle. The puzzle has been first laid at a very young age. When only a few pieces are put, it's hard to tell what the whole puzzle will look like. In essence, that puzzle has stopped working and is sitting in the same spot with no further pieces assembled. It was kind of completely forgotten. It's a secret that's only between God and me.

Obviously, the goal or plan that was made in my young age was absolutely different from the lesson of completely surrendering before God, which is Pastor McGrew's biblical viewpoint. He said that God gives us what's the best for us, not what we want. These two issues are extremely different, and they are very far apart from each other. *How can I face or handle them?* I was wondering!

I want to be honest to say that I grew up with no-self, false-self in my childhood. I believe that we are all products of our environments, such as family in origin, clans of surroundings, social media, habitual and cultural background, etc. In reality, some of the aspects or factors have more influence than others. Psychologically, they are different based on each individual's growing stages, in general.

After we bought the house in Skokie Village, Illinois. It is just the next city to Chicago. I didn't know why I wanted to go to school but only part-time and still working full-time back then. The question was, "What should I take?" My husband told me to take computer science—easy to get a job and pay is good. That's true and practical. In fact, most of the female students who came to US from

Taiwan, that's what they studied. But for me, it definitely wasn't computer science because I have no interest at all. Then I started to pray, "Dear Lord, God, You knew that I wanted to go to school, and since I want to obey Your will, I want to take what You want me to take, not what I want regardless. I want to major in the field which you want me to take, not for money, or anything else. The focal point is that I won't take anything but only take what you want me to, nothing else—period! So please let me know. Thank You for listening to my prayers."

I have been praying every single day continually for two weeks in a row. Two weeks later, on Sunday, during the break between Sunday school and the service, while I was talking with someone, at the same time, I saw a lady who was also talking with someone just about four, five feet from me. While I was talking, I heard that her conversation partner had asked her a question. "Rivera, what's your major in your graduate program?"

She answered, "Guidance and counseling."

Interestingly enough, the moment I heard that, I told myself, "That's it! That's exactly also what I want for myself."

Honestly, if someone had asked me then, "What's that?" my true answer for sure would've been, "I don't know!" because I really didn't know.

Question: "How could you decide on something if you don't even know what it is and make a decision immediately without thinking and hesitation?" In this regard, the only answer was from the Holy Spirit. It was God who put that desire in my heart to decide, and He orchestrated the chance of hearing from that lady's conversation. "Delight yourself in the Lord, and He'll put His desire into your heart" (Psalm 37:4). Another good one to confirm: "For the Holy Spirit will teach you at that time" (Luke 12:12 I paraphrased). I believe that those two verses are very much depicting the episodes.

Afterward, when I was in the class, we were asked why we were taking this class. My answer was, "If I were a fish, you put me in the water because that's where I belong." I didn't know what's the reason, in real essence, I felt very sure that I simply loved and enjoyed studying psychology courses. Those textbooks to me, I felt like I was reading a love story when I was a teenager. I couldn't put it down, even kind of obsessed with it, and I always wanted to study more and more. Simply amazing! Honestly, there were times I simply couldn't stop until 1:00, 2:00, or even after 3:00 a.m. because I always said, "One more page," "Another page" on and on until physically worn out or my brain shut down.

I remember Pastor Chuck Swindoll on his teaching about how to discover your spiritual gifts. The first principle on the list is *interesting*. I think that is exactly matching mine.

In real essence, at first, I wasn't going to get the degree. I just love to study for my own sake, doing something that I simply enjoy to do. I enjoy what I read and feel a sense of satisfaction. In effect, they truly cherished and nourished my inner being. It's so true that:

> True fulfillment comes from loving what you do.
> (Matt Damon, producer, actor, Oscar winner)

> Being able to wake up every day and do the things you loved was the pinnacle of success.
> (Steve Jobs, cofounder, Apple)

I say amen with them.

Indeed, during the process of my study journey, it was very difficult and hard. When I studied the textbooks, simply reading those professional words or terminology matter already driving me crazy and stressed me out. However, the hardships still didn't stop me or knock me down. I still persistently, continually went for it. Thanks to God, those hardships or obstacles couldn't stop me. In effect, the enjoyment and rewards actually were far more than the hardships I had been through. If I didn't overcome the hardships patiently and persistently, I wouldn't have made it through to the end. "No pain, no gain"—I think this is very true! At this moment, I just vividly remember when we were still kids. My mother always said to us that the only way to achieve your goal is to go through the hard times. Regardless, same idea, same principal!

Regarding taking the comprehensive test, there was also an amazing, interesting story. In order to get a degree, I must take this test. In fact, it wasn't my plan to get the degree at first, but I simply kept on studying. Before I knew it, I had just about finished the whole program. Therefore, I might just finish all of them. I even turned in the thesis before I moved to Riverside.

About three, four months later, I received a letter from my school that I had to take the comprehensive test in order to complete the graduate program. The dean of the Psychology Department informed me that she will mail the test to UCR instead of back to Chicago, so for my convenience, I can take the test at UCR. I was told on the phone that the test will be sent to UCR. About a week or so, I have to contact a staff in the Education Department.

This next story is a bizarre and strange story about sending the test from my school in Chicago to UCR, in Riverside, California. We were expected to receive the test about a week after we were told, but we didn't. We waited for a couple more days. Still no test. The lady in the education department in UCR had to call my school to send the second test, and they did. However, the same thing happened to the second test. It also took about two weeks of waiting and yielded the same result: no test. The same thing happened to both tests, and nobody knew why. I simply think it's strange and bewildering!

I will make this story brief. When the school sent the first test and second test, I was waiting a total of four weeks but still didn't get the paper. Finally, left with no other choice, the lady in UCR called (and I did too) and asked for the third one. They did send it, but guess what? Again, strangely and interestingly, it took longer than one week. It was finally received within two weeks. UCR finally received the test, the third one. At the time I was checking on the delivery progress, in those conversations between the two of us, both of us totally agreed that this incident was really unusual and strange. The last time I called her about an update on the test, she spoke to me, "That's a really unusual incident." It took about 6, or 7 weeks in a row, yet still no mail. In fact, they had to send it the third time, and finally a week later, we got the test. The lady finally said to me,

"Yolanda, maybe there was a reason for this unusually delaying mail! Maybe you need more time to study."

That's it! Perfect comment! Bingo! How did she figure it out? In effect, that's exactly the whole point. As a matter of fact, during that waiting time, there was a family from Chicago visiting us, staying in our house. The couple had five children. The couple were busy looking for work. I was the housewife, cooking for seven people and buying grocery, and even took the boy to school daily. That was a heavy load of daily work. I didn't mean to complain, but it was a reality. I had a good reason that I couldn't study. That's why the lady in UCR said to me, "Maybe there's a reason for the mail being delayed for so long!" That's exactly the story behind it, but how did she know? As for me, I thought God used this way and gave me extra time to study because I needed it.

The six, or seven weeks of waiting for the test, it finally came to pass. The lady from UCR told me specifically where to go, to park my car, and the room to take my test. Amazingly enough, I want to describe another interesting episode while I was walking to the designated room from my parking place. I walked at least five, seven minutes. I was totally calm, easy, not nervous at all. What's wrong with me?

I remember from back to schooltime, we had a saying, "Small test, small nervous. Big test, big nervous!" This was the biggest and most important test to me. How come I wasn't fearful? At least I should feel nervous, especially since I wasn't quite reviewed enough as I should. I had every reason to feel worried and nervous, yet the reality was "didn't even feel nervous!" As we always say and believe, we can only do the best, and God will take care of the rest. There's a scripture matching this episode perfectly: "God won't let you carry the burden more than you can. When that situation happens, He will help you to find a way out" (1 Corinthians 10:13 I paraphrased). This was just another evidence to prove God's faithful provision and promises.

At last, the staff gave me the test and told me, "You have two hours." When I first opened it, there were five big questions, except one of the questions that I thought I knew, and the rest of them I didn't quite understand weren't fully clear. Yet still didn't even feel nervous and fear at all. I started answering the questions according to the order. I didn't have time to think. I just kept on writing nonstop. Honestly, I didn't have time to think, and I didn't know what I was writing. I only knew that I had to hurry to work on it.

Finally, the second that I put down my pen, the lady walked in and told me that time was up, and she took my paper away. I felt that I couldn't even have time to breathe during the test. I thought my brain was about to blow up and explode. The result of the test didn't turn out very good, but the good news was I passed the test.

In the end, despite all of the ups and downs, I finally completely finished it. I was conferred a degree of master of arts in guidance and counseling from Northeastern Illinois University in Chicago, Illinois. In effect, I actually learned and saw that from all of those small incidents, here or there, I simply did the very best I could. As a result, God really took care perfectly to complete the rest.

I want to humbly and sincerely give all the praises and glory to Him alone! I knew for a fact that without God's working on every situation—small or big steps, every turn, etc.—He had been behind the scenes at all times from the very beginning.

About six or eight months later, Northern Illinois University in DeKalb, Illinois, sent me a letter and offered me a full scholarship to work on a PhD degree in psychology. I humbly felt that was a great honor and privilege to me. I didn't take it because our daughter's adoption process was just about to come to pass. I chose to be a full-time stay-at-home mother and homemaker.

In regard to fulfilling the private wish in my young age, time flies. Life's been very tough and challenging just about my whole life. That desire or wish had been completely out of my mind and even totally had been forgotten. Yet in essence, God has perfect memory. He always knows what He's doing. He has been guiding me, directing me to the directions that He wanted me to head on. From time to time while I was walking off the track, He always guided me back to the right track and moved to only the direction that He guided or prepared for me.

During the process of the journey, there were so many numerous amazing and strange detours and unexpected radical turns that I didn't even know during the turning process and procedures. However, in the end, He perpetually orchestrated His perfect plan and has brought me to the place where precisely and exactly was what I originally had been committed to myself at a very young age. As I mentioned earlier, nobody knew that secret; it was only between God and me. As a matter of fact, now I want to tell the actual incident behind the secret story, or the "unfinished puzzle" issue. This incident sounds very small, unimportant talking in a way, the kind of talking, nothing special, just between the parents and their kids talking and interactions. It happened when I was in the second or third grade. One day, out of the blue, my father, who had proudly shown me and my siblings the first-place certificate he received in his class, said to us, "Someday, I wish you guys can do this too. Someday, when you guys grow up, [remember that] those who have more money should help those who have less." Ever since, I have made up my mind to achieve those two particular goals at that young age. Amazingly, I don't know why those two key factors immediately took root deep within my heart then.

As I mentioned earlier, just like the illustration of the puzzle that was only a few pieces put out, and couldn't tell what it was back then.

Sometimes I wonder, *How come that at such a young, pure, innocent age, I was able to come up with that kind of idea or future plan in my mind?* Honestly, I don't understand either. The only way I could think is that the scripture says it well: "It is the pure in heart who see God" (Matthew 6:8). Obviously, the only answer to that question is that the Word of God convicted me deeply because it's all part of the divine design, a grand plan of the future journey in my life.

In fact, to this very day, I am still tending to my father's two great concerns. Regarding helping others, I don't only help my family members. I also help my relatives and others who are in need. I consider it a great blessing and honor. In so doing, I give thanks to the Lord for being able to do so. The Bible says it's more blessed to give than receive (Acts 20:35). I also believe that the Spirit-filled Christians always do good deeds out of compassion, not compulsion. When we were kids and all the way up to adulthood, we unanimously couldn't deny that our father has been sacrificing and generously helping other people in need at all times in his life. We also weren't in good shape financially. He had to work very hard to put the food on the table for fourteen people. His actions spoke louder than his words. I believe that also played significant factor that impacted my life.

Through it all, in the end, God, in His miraculous ways, graciously gave me the ability and opportunities to do so. Thank You, Lord. Ultimately, it's YOU alone who orchestrated and fulfilled Your faithful promises on those complicated but beautiful and awesome stories. Thank You, Lord, for being such a faithful provider. It signified the evidence for what Pastor McGrew had said to me in the beginning, "When you pray, God gives you what's the best, but not what you want." Yes, indeed. So very true!

*Final conclusion*

Our life is God's story. As McGrew said before, God has a grand plan for each one of us. In effect, my two most important desires in my life were not the best things for me at all. Through it all, I finally could see the whole picture of God's intentional grand plan for me in the very beginning. It's absolutely amazing. Everything Pastor McGrew had said in our house was confirmed and came to pass amazingly one by one.

To be honest, before I came to the US, I have to confess that I didn't like to read the Bible. I always thought that the Bible is boring to me. Miraculously, it started when I first went to Pastor McGrew's church, it happened on the first Sunday service. Honestly, I don't remember the content of his sermon. All I remember is that after the service, I suddenly felt changed dramatically, and I felt it was the Spirit transforming me and awakening me deep within my heart. As the song "Amazing Grace," goes, "how sweet the sound… was blind but now I see." The words of the song and their meaning exactly depict my emotional and spiritual state. I also realized that I could see His Word in my spirit eyes. That radical change made me extremely joyful and thrilled. Since then, every time I sing or hum to this song to myself, I just can't stop in tears. Those words very much describe my situation. It's by the grace of God that He opened my spiritual eyes to see *who* He really is. Thank You, Lord, for deepening my desire, guiding me to Your will, and helping me stay in the will you set for me. It's been a great blessing that You've given me the hungering and longing heart for Your Word to this very day. It's simply the greatest *blessing* in my life. It matches what Pastor McGrew said before, "God gives you what's the best for you, but not what you want." Thank You, Lord, for bringing me back to the *right* track when I once was lost and wandering.

Pastor John Dixon of Crest Community Church in Riverside, California, once he has asked me that psychology major in grad school, how did that affect me in my life? Excellent question! That's the specific major that God wanted me to take. So what's the purpose for taking that major? The answer is it's everything to do in my whole life journey.

God Almighty knows exactly what He's doing. He knew me before I was even born (Psalm 129:16). Seriously, the simple answer, it did tremendously work from transforming to affirming. I will share the details some other time. Let's start with the family I was born into. I grew up in an unhealthy, dysfunctional family. Besides the non-Christian environment and unhealthy cultural backgrounds, among other things, God knows my weaknesses, frailties, and unhealthy personality in many respects. A psychology major was exactly what I needed the most besides the *Word* of God. Studying psychology is also one of the spiritual gifts God has given to me. Apparently, I didn't know myself until I got into the program. According to the Bible, the purpose of the spiritual gift is only to edify the believers and glorify the name of the Lord (1 Corinthians 14). Therefore, studying psychology impacted me a great deal, regarding changing and improving my unhealthy, codependent personality. In addition, I believe that was part of God's way to equip me and train me to be an effective and mature vessel for the future ministry in my life. In real essence,

Besides the Word of God, I think that I have devoted to learn and study more about psychological knowledge and wisdom to examine myself and human relationships. In so doing, I seek knowledge from books, using good resources, which I thought was very helpful for me to handle and face all kinds of conflicts in my life's journey in general, in addition, of course, with God's powerful Word and strength. I have been more comfortable and boldly speaking the truth in love (Ephesians 4:15). The Moody's study guide says the same thing. Those who receive God's Word must be faithful in sharing them even when they are hard to say. With that great insight rekindled, it encouraged me more boldly to put in into action.

As a Christian, I don't want to be phony or pretend. I have always been a good, naive person but was unhealthy in some psychological respects and issues. As a result, my self-esteem was polluted, affected by the carnal way of life. I didn't know why after I went to Pastor McGrew's church, immediately I developed a strong desire have had the spiritual craving heart and longing for God's *Word*. This was unprecedented situation, it had never happened before in my life. I'd say that's a mystery to me even to this very day. Ever since, my life has been dramatically changed and different. Gradually and slowly, I realized that I should only live for Jesus, who died for me. As the scripture said, "If anyone is in Christ, he is a new creation; the old one has gone, the new one has come" (2 Corinthians 5:15–17). Ironically, the only one thing that can change me and truly set me free is based on His *Word*. "You shall know the truth, and the truth will set you free, indeed" (John 8:32 I paraphrased). Therefore, studying the psychology field is just part of God's way as His tool to reshape me, redirect me from my previous whole life's unhealthy patterns.

For at least several decades, I have been diligently, constantly having the desire or love to read and study the scriptures and wanting to learn good resources about psychological and emotional issues as well. Even to this very day, untiringly, I considered that a blessing. I didn't know why I was always feeling real joy and true satisfaction in my heart. Dr. Chuck Swindoll's radio teaching with the study guide was my first powerful study foundation or experience. I especially appreciate him and Dr. James Dobson; I considered both of them my early ministers and mentors because I benefited greatly from their teachings and ministries.

Timewise, in general, I sometimes go with Moody Bible Institute's devotional guide and a few other good resources. However, I mostly stick with one of my favorites—radio ministry with Pastor Jon Courson. His teachings are also very in-depth and applicable. I have also taken about forty or so credits from the ministry of Caring for People God's way and had received a certificate as a member of the American Association of Christian Counselors (AACC). All of those professional teachings are combining the theological truth and their professional knowledge and wisdom. Their sound, truthful teachings have been a blessing to me. I have been nourished and cherished, and I really have grown a great deal thanks to their ministry.

I believe that they were God's intentional ways for me to be developed, changed, and grown. As Pastor Swindoll said that is the self-taught, self-study. I am a slow learner but are perpetual diligent enthusiastic nonstop learner. I think that's God giving spiritual gifts, I consider it as a great blessing.

On the other hand, besides to credit God for His divine help at all times through so many powerful resources, I want to especially give thanks to a very special person who, I should say, is the most influential person who virtually impacted my life the most. Mrs. Meggie Borah, a beautiful Irish artist lady. She practically was the person whom God has placed to be as a mother figure to me. At first, we lived close as neighbors and gradually became good friends and have built good relationships as family. She actually played a combination of roles as a mother, sister, best friend, English teacher, counselor or psychologist, and an attentive listener as well. I have been very blessed to have such a loving, kind, wonderful, special person in my life for almost thirty years until the Lord called her home. Life without her, I felt great loss, loneliness, and grief in my heart for a long time. There were precious, sweet memory. There were so many times she was sitting on the rocking bench under the big tree in her front yard, and I was sitting on the swinger hanging under the same big tree. Those are my free-of-charge counseling or therapy sessions.

There were some unforgettable precious memories or moments. Sometimes, we shared some of life's tough-time issues in tears and laughed out loud to tears. Other times, we even talked some silly, stupid crazy or funny jokes. As I write this, I can't stop saying while in tears, "Meggie, I love you and miss you very much. Life without you around is really different. I feel sorry for myself, but I am glad that you are in the perfect place God prepared for you! You will always be missed in my heart!" Her comments are always the same: "Yolanda, that's funny. You made my day." We really had good times and enjoyed being with each other. We both had two things in common besides loving duck very much. One time, she actually baked a whole duck just for me. I was deeply touched. Nobody has ever done that for me and cared for me like her.

Another thing in common: we both are genuine, simple, truthful people. At some points, I was surprised that she understood me more than I did. That's another point I knew for a fact. On one hand, God has used her to remake me for who I am in some respects. On the other hand, I believe God has placed her to be a mother figure in my life because I needed one.

The encountering story with Mrs. Maggie Borah has been one of the greatest blessing. It was all through this very special dream home on Spruce Street, which God particularly provided for my family, especially for me. It wasn't only a once-and-done incident or story. It has been a continuing journey through my whole life span even to this day. It is not only a house, it's a very special place that God purposely, intentionally reserved for me, a place where I have been experiencing God's actual presence in a tangible way, a place where I feel I belong in my lifetime.

At the same time, it's also a place that God used for another good purpose. Who would've known that after my children had moved out of the house, my kitchen and living room would become a place for those people who feel comfortable and willing to open their hearts, sharing their inner issues and feelings of joy and pains as well. I don't know why, but for some reason, those people who have gone through tough times or are struggling with depression or other emotional issues seem to like to come to me; I feel that they like to come to me to share about their life. For instance (and this is true), there were a few people who have said to me, "If you don't listen to me now, I will die. There's no one that I can't talk to or who will listen to me." And that would be the time that I'd witness to them about Jesus! Ultimately, He is the real healer and rescuer. Without Him, I wouldn't be who I am now. Regardless of their religion, I am glad that I was that someone available to them at that desperate moments.

As I have said previously, Christianity is like a beggar telling the other beggars where to find the *best* food: *the gospel.* That's exactly matching this scriptures: "God of all comforts…who comforts us in all our troubles, so that we can comfort those in any troubles with the comforts we ourselves have received from God" (2 Corinthians 1:3, 4 I paraphrased). That's the perfect scripture describing or depicting all the stories in my ministry. In effect, having had Meggie Borah so close in my life, it was strictly connected with this house. When the adoption news was on newspaper, Maggie was the first person who brought a gift to our daughter.

On the other hand, who would've known that later on, it would become a place for many hurting people to share their stories both good and bad, etc. So the key element in all these incidents were everything to do with this particular house on Spruce Street. As I think it through, I should ultimately thank God for His intentional plan for me. Just as the story details said, we wouldn't be able to live in this meaningful house. There were other crucial episodes as well, such as being able to bring our daughter to the US in a dramatic way and to have had Mrs. Meggie Borah be part as my special friend—all credited to this "dream home," which was provided for us, for me.

All of the encounters were simply for the purpose of fulfilling God's intentional grand plan for me in my whole life. The beauty was that it started from the most significant and basic lesson of *completely surrendering before God.* Ironically, that key element began and ended at the same focal point. For my part was simply absolutely obeying and submitting to His will and plan without even worrying about what's ahead and whether I understood it or not. In essence, as always, He practically and actually takes care of everything in His way and in His time. Sometime later I will find out and realize in due time.

Now, I would like to wrap them up with these four relatively evident verses to conclude this story.

> Delight yourself in the Lord, and He will put His desire in your heart. (Psalm 37:4)

> What I have said, that will I bring about; what I have planned, that will I do. (Isaiah 46:11b)

> He who began the good work, will carry on to the completion. (Philippians 1:6)

Those powerful *words* of God actually prove God's faithfulness always regardless! The last one: "God won't let you carry the burden more than you are able. When that happens, He will help you to find a way out" (1 Corinthians 10:13).

I want to wrap up with a few principals that describe this whole article. It all started from a simple, casual visit from Pastor McGrew at our house. We had a good time conversing. Everything he said was meant to be the main significant issues in our life journey. When I look back slowly, I ponder on whether he was an angel God sent to our house. I strongly believe that everything he said was part of God's grand plan, laid and pre-told to us through him.

The following powerful insights were what he said to us:

1. As a Christian, our first and foremost lesson to learn or pray about is completely surrendering before God, not for a child or anything else.
2. When you pray, God gives you what's best for you, not what you want.
3. God answers our prayers according to His ways and His timetable.
4. Since we all worship the same God, someday, we will all go to the same God. So what's the difference between your child and my child?

These were the rock-solid biblical "golden rules" to me in my whole life journey, even to this very day and the future, until the Lord calls me home.

I am still learning slowly, falling, tumbling, and struggling from time to time.

Thank God for Pastor McGrew's powerful biblical encouragement. I believe I took those words to heart; they are roots planted deep within me. Some of them, I only remember as my head knowledge. The only key element is that we simply can't do it on our own but through the *Word* of God and by His spirit. The *Word* is Jesus Himself (John 1: 1). The point is that the Spirit-filled life is inextricably linked to the Word. In other words, being filled with the Spirit and being filled with the Word are linked together.

Lastly, I'd like to quote my favorite great insight and/or perspective from Dr. Charles Swindoll.

> The longer I live, the more I realize the impact of attitude on life. Attitude, to me, is more important than fact. It is more important than the past, than education, than money, than circumstances, than failures, than success, than what other people think or say or do. It is more important than appearance, giftedness, or skill. It will make or break a company...at church...at home. The remarkable thing is we have a choice every day regarding the attitude we will embrace for that day. We cannot change our past. We cannot change the inevitable. The only thing is our attitude. I am convinced that life is 10% what happens to me and 90% how I react to it. And so it is with you...we are in charge of our attitudes.

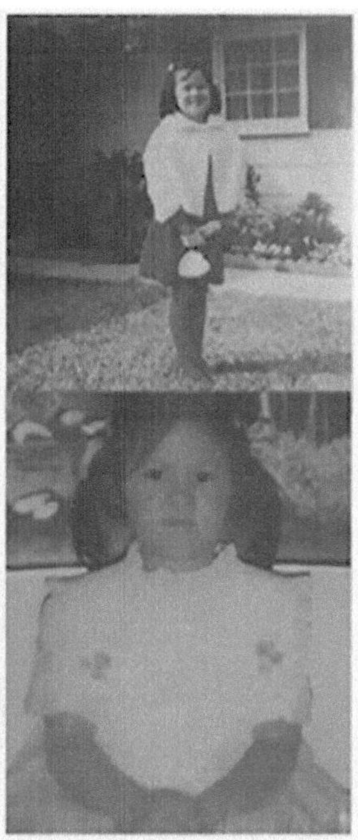

# About the Author

One day, I was reading a devotional guide, and it said, "Wisdom cries out to the 'dumb, simple, naive, and unsophisticated people.'" I said to myself that's exactly describing me. How interesting! I think I fit every one of those characteristics. In my life, I have experienced firsthand the deep conviction by the Holy Spirit and sensed the call from God to write those God-given amazing stories. As a result, as a beggar who tasted firsthand, and with a burning desire to share with other beggars where to find the "best food," the gospel of Jesus. May all those remarkable stories serve as a light shining through wherever God leads or directs.

Thank you for reading my stories.